The Pec

INVERNESS
at Home and Abroad
1800 - 1850

By David Dobson

CLEARFIELD

Published for Clearfield Company by
Genealogical Publishing Company
Baltimore, Maryland
2022

ISBN: 9780806359410

Introduction

The book contains references to people from Inverness-shire, at home and abroad, between 1800 and 1850. The entries bring together emigrants and their destinations-- especially in North America, the West Indies, and Australasia--with their kin who remained in Scotland. Inverness-shire itself was, and continues to be a bastion of Gaeldom, and the home of several important clans, such as the McKenzies, the Frasers, the Grants, the McIntoshes, the McPhersons, the McGillivrays, the McBeans, the McQueens, the Davidsons, and other members of Clan Chattan. The burgh of Inverness was the administrative and commercial centre for the county of Inverness-shire; it was, and is, a major route centre for road and rail traffic. The population of the burgh was around 10,000 people in 1800 and rose to around 13,000 by mid-century.

Ehe information herein is derived from a wide range of sources such as court records, contemporary newspapers and journals, monumental inscriptions, and documents found in archives. Three published sources are worthy of special mention. The Statistical Report of Scotland, originated by Sir John Sinclair, is a collection of reports by nearly one thousand Scottish parish ministers compiled between 1791 and 1799. These reports cover a wide range of topics for each parish, including geography, education, history, agriculture, shipping, population, and religious denominations. The O.S.A. is therefore a unique source of useful background for the family historian as it provides an insight to Scottish society at the end of the eighteenth century. The Highland Clearances, from the mid-18th to the mid-19th century, caused a rural depopulation and a diaspora south to Lowland Scotland, England, North America, and Australasia. Rapid changes in Scottish society with the Agricultural Revolution and the Industrial Revolution resulted in the New Statistical Report being researched between 1832 and 1845. Both the O.S.A. and New Statistical Report were published and may be found in most of the older libraries in Scotland; however, they are both available online on the website of the National Library of Scotland. Finally, the publications of the Gaelic Society of Inverness cover a wide range of topics, both in Gaelic and English, most of which should be of interest to the family historian. All three of these published sources should enable researchers with roots in Inverness-shire to put their family into a historical context.

David Dobson, Dundee, Scotland, 2022

REFERENCES

AJ   Aberdeen Journal, series

AMC   Annals of Megantic County, Quebec

ANY   St Andrew's Society of New York

BA   Officers of the Bengal Army

BPP   British Parliamentary Papers

C   Canna, [Edinburgh, 1994]

CD   Clan Donald

CM   Caledonian Mercury, series

CMM   Clan MacMillan Magazine, series

DCPA   Dundee, Perth and Cupar Advertiser, series

DFpp   Duncan Fraser papers, Montgomery County Archives, N.Y.

EA   Edinburgh Advertiser, series

EC   Edinburgh Courant, series

EEC   Edinburgh Evening Courant, series

F   Fasti Ecclesiae Scoticanae, [Edinburgh]

GA   Glasgow Advertiser, series

GC   Glasgow Courier, series

GkAd   Greenock Advertiser, series

GM   Gentleman's Magazine, series

GSP   Glasgow Saturday Post, series

HBRS   Hudson Bay Record Society

HJ Halifax Journal, series

HT Halifax Times, series

HOFL History of the Frasers of Lovat

HS History Scotland, series

IC Inverness Courier, series

INC Index of North Carolina Ancestors

IPR Inverness Poor Register, [Highland Archives, BI.4.1.32a]

KCA King's College, Aberdeen

MCA Marischal College, Aberdeen

NARA National Archives Records Administration

NBC New Brunswick Courier, series

NCSA North Carolina State Archives

NLS National Library of Scotland

NRS National Records of Scotland

PAC Public Archives of Canada

PAO Pubic Archives of Ontario

PAPEI Public Archives of Prince Edward Island

QCG Quebec City Gazette

RSA Rose-Steel Anthology

S The Scotsman, series

SCA Scottish Catholic Archives

SCA South Carolina Archives

SG   Scottish Guardian, series

SM   Scots Magazine, series

TNA   The National Archives

TSA   The Scots in America

W   Witness, series

WRHS   Western Reserve Historical Society

PLAN.
of the Town of
INVÈRNESS.

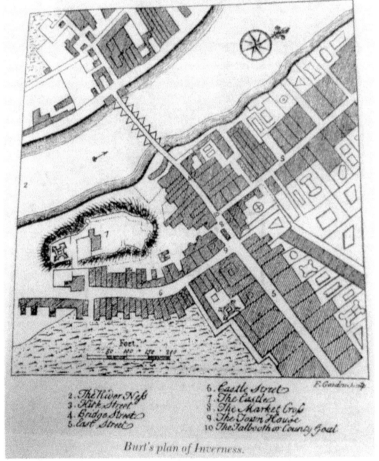

2. The River Neß
3. Kirk Street
4. Bridge Street
5. East Street
6. Castle Street
7. The Castle
8. The Market Cross
9. The Town House
10. The Talbooth or County Goal

F. Gordon. sc.

Burt's plan of Inverness.

A Highland Clearance

A Lochside Religious Service

Highland Line with Clan Identifications

Highlanders in Highland Scenery

x

Processing Wool

Country Dance

Urquhart Castle

Muckrach Castle

Ruthven Castle

Eilean Donald Castle

Inverness on the River Ness

THE PEOPLE OF INVERNESS AT HOME AND ABROAD 1800-1850

ADAMSON, DONALD, a pedlar in Moidart, [Muideart], emigrated via Druimindarroch on board the Jane bound for Prince Edward Island in July 1790. [SCA]

AITKEN, MARK, minister of the united parish of Dyke and Moy, 1821. [NRS.GD2.270]

ALEXANDER, ADAM, born 1758 in Inverness, studied medicine in Edinburgh, emigrated to America, a surgeon in the Continental Army, married Louisa Frederika Schmidt in 1802, parents of Adam Leopold Alexander, born 1803, died 1883. [Duke University, cab.81.1940]

ALLARDYCE, JAMES, from Inverness, graduated MA from King's College, Aberdeen, in March 1834, later minister at Bowden. [KCA]

ALVES, ALEXANDER, second son of Dr John Alves a physician in Inverness, died in Jamaica in 1796. [EEC.12278]

ALVES, HELEN, daughter of Dr John Alves a physician in Inverness, [Inphir Nis], married George Inglis from Demerara, in Springfield on 24 July 1798. [SM.60.575]

ALVES, JAMES, born 1737, a portrait painter, died in Inverness on 27 November 1808. [AJ.21.12.1808]

ALVES, THOMAS, of Shipland, a merchant in Inverness, dead by 1792. [NRS.S/H]

ANDERSON, ALEXANDER, in Castle Street, Inverness, a victim of housebreaking and theft in 1830. [NRS.AD14.30.81]

ANDERSON, ALEXANDER MACKENZIE, born 1830, a Lieutenant in the Bengal Establishment of the East India Company, died in Inverness on 31 July 1857. [Chapel Yard gravestone, Inverness]

ANDERSON, ARCHIBALD, from Inverness, graduated MA from King's College, Aberdeen, in 1816, later minister of Crathie. [KCA]

1

ANDERSON, BENJAMIN GASKIN, of Tushielaw, a sasine of land in the barony of Moy in 1837. [NRS.GD1.1003.82]

ANDERSON, or MCRAE, BETSEY, born 1800 in Urray, a pauper in McIntosh's Close, Green, Inverness in 1857. [IPR]

ANDERSON, Mrs ELIZABETH, born 1792, died 18 March 1869, widow of Colonel Sir Alexander Anderson. [Brachlich gravestone]

ANDERSON, JANET, widow of John Baillie a goldsmith in Inverness, testament, 29 September 1800, Comm. Inverness. [NRS]

ANDERSON, JOHN, born 1748, died in Invergarry on 4 May 1832. [Kilchuimen gravestone]

ANDERSON, JOHN, born 1797, tacksman of Lagnalien, died on 18 December 1879, husband of Christian McDonald, born 1798, died 13 March 1873. [Old High gravestone, Inverness]

ANDERSON, KATHERINE, spouse of Alexander Livingston a baker in Inverness, testament, 29 September 1800, Comm. Inverness. [NRS]

ANDERSON, ROBERT, a goldsmith in Inverness from 1755 to his death in 1792, son of James Anderson of Knocknagiel, testament, 20 October 1800, Comm. Inverness. [NRS]

ANDERSON, VIOLET ALEXANDRA, in Clymer, Oregon, heir to her great-grandmother Isobel Noble, widow of Alexander Anderson at Culloden Muir, who died in 1854, re property in Queen Street, Inverness. [NRS.S/H]

ANDERSON, or MACPHERSON, WILLIAMINA, born 1789 in Inverness, a pauper in Huntly Street, Inverness, in 1857. [IVR]

ANDREWS, ELIZA, in Daviot Park, Swan River, Manitoba, a letter to James Grant of Bucht enquiring about her mother and sisters in 1835. [NRS.GD23.6707]

ANGUS, ALEXANDER, born 1730, died at Moss-side of Mounie, Daviot, on 5 December 1825. [SM.97.128]

ANGUS, PETER, master of the Start of Inverness trading with Easdale in 1825, [NRS.E504.17.9]

ANNARD, ELIZABETH, widow of John McIntosh of Culclachy, testament, 20 January 1791, Comm. Inverness. [NRS]

ARBUCKLE, JOHN, from Inverness, graduated MA from King's College, Aberdeen, in March 1818. [KCA]

AUSTIN, HUGH, hostler to Donald Cameron an innkeeper in Fort William, was found guilty of assault and was sentenced to two months imprisonment in 1821. [NRS.JC26.1821.112]

BAILLIE, GEORGE, from Inverness, graduated MA from King's College, Aberdeen, on 26 April 1813, later a surgeon in the Service of the East India Company. [KCA]

BAILLIE, HELEN, born 1785 in Inverness, a pauper in Tomnahurich Street, Inverness, in 1857. [IPR]

BAILLIE, JOHN, a farmer in Inverness, father of Francis Baillie a sailor in the Royal Navy in 1799. [NRS.S/H]

BAILLIE, JOHN, from Inverness, Professor of Arab and Persian Literature at Fort William, Bengal, graduated as a Doctor of Laws from King's College, Aberdeen, on 11 October 1803. [KCA]

BAIN, DONALD, a merchant in Inverness in 1811. [NRS.E504.17.8]

BAIN, DONALD, born 1744, died in Inverness on 15 December 1825. [SM.97.128]

BAIN, DONALD, born 1798, a wood merchant in Inverness, died 29 June 1838, husband of Jessie Noble, born 1800, died 6 September 1851. [Chapel Yard gravestone, Inverness]

BAIN, HUGH, born 1791, from Strathglass, emigrated via Fort William aboard the Sarah of Liverpool bound for Pictou, Nova Scotia, in June 1801. [NRS.RH2.4.87]

BAIN, or MCKENZIE, ISABELLA, born 1770 in Inverness, a servant now a pauper in Kessock Street, Inverness, in 1857, mother of John born 1817, a blacksmith now abroad, William born 1819 now in Australia, etc. [IPR]

BAIN, or MCINTOSH, ISABELLA, born 1801 in Urquhart daughter of John McIntosh, a widow and a pauper in Green of Muirtown in 1857. [IPR]

BAIN, or FRASER, MARY, born 1767 in Inverness, a widow, a former servant, and a pauper in Beaton's Close, Inverness, in 1857, died 1859. [IPR]

BAIN, PETER, [1825-1908], and his wife Jane Grigor, [1827-1908], parents of Jessie Bain born 1852, died in USA on 30 June 1890. [Urquhart gravestone]

BAIN, THOMAS, from Inverness, graduated MA from King's College, Aberdeen, on 31 January 1807, later Rector of Fortrose Academy. [KCA]

BAIN, WILLIAM, master of the Rosamond of Fort William trading with Lerwick and Inverness in 1823. [NRS.E504.17.9]

BAIN, WILLIAM, born 1779 in Kiltarlity, a widower, former soldier of the 50th Regiment, now a pauper in Beaton's Lane, Glebe Street, Inverness in 1857. [IPR]

BARCLAY, JOHN, born 24 October 1787 in Tain, a Major of the Bengal Cavalry, died in Inverness on 13 December 1843. [Chapel Yard gravestone, Inverness]

BARRON, RODERICK, born 1785, died 29 August 1864, husband of Anne MacPherson, born 1784, died 31 October 1861, parents of Alexander, Roderick, James, and John – all of whom died in South America, also of Donald Barron in Dores. [Dores gravestone]

BARRON, WILLIAM, born 1780 in Kirkhill, husband of Christian Calder born 1797 in Kilmorack, paupers in Nelson Street, Inverness, in 1857. [IPR]

BATHGATE, ARCHIBALD, born 1810, a stockman from Inverness, with his wife Christian, and children, Nancy born 1829, John born 1831, Alexander born 1833, Archibald born 1835, and Adam born 1837, emigrated via Greenock aboard the William Rodger, master John Reid, landed in New South Wales on 26 September 1838. [NSWpa]

BAYNE, CHARLES JOHN, from Inverness, graduated MA from King's College, Aberdeen, in March 1817, later minister at Fodderty. [KCA]

BAYNE, JAMES, son of Ronald Bayne in Inverness, a student in Marischal College around 1800, graduated MA in 1805, and MD in 1811. [MCA][KCA]

BEAN, GEORGE, born 1722, a writer in Inverness, died on 16 March 1798. [Chapel Yard gravestone, Inverness]

BEATON, ALEXANDER, Baron Baillie of Urquhart, died at Allanmore on 15 December 1825. [SM.97.128]

BEATON, or MACKENZIE, JANET, born 1814 in Inverness, a widow, a former servant and a pauper in King Street, Inverness, in 1857. [IPR]

5

BEATON, or FRASER, JEAN, born 1797 in Kirkhill, a widow, a domestic servant now a pauper in Pumpgate Street, Inverness, in 1857, mother of Peter born 1830 now in USA. [IPR]

BEATON, WILLIAM, from Inverness, graduated MA from King's College, Aberdeen, on 31 March 1827. [KCA]

BEATSON, ALEXANDER, born 1824, with Margaret Beatson born 1825, from Marishader, Skye, emigrated via Liverpool aboard the Ticonderoga bound for Port Philip, Australia, on 4 August 1852. [NRS.HD4/5]

BENNET, ISAAC, son of Robert Bennet in Fort George, died in Belvidere Estate, St Thomas in the East, Jamaica in 1800. [AJ.2720][GC1324]

BENNET, ROBERT, baptised 11 May 1758, in Fort George, Ardesier, son of Robert Bennet and his wife Agnes McIntosh, a mariner who was naturalised in South Carolina on 13 April 1805. [NARA.M1183.1]; died in Charleston, S.C., on 19 October 1816. [Old Scots gravestone, Charleston] [Charleston City Gazette: 31.10.1816]

BETHUNE, or MACKAY, MARGARET, born 1781 in Inverness, a pauper and a widow in Fraser's Close, Inverness, in 1857. [IPR]

BETHUNE, MARION, born 1800, daughter Anne born 1825, son Murdoch born 1828, daughter Christy born 1833, son Roderick born 1841, and daughter Ann born 1838, from Uig, Skye, emigrated via Liverpool aboard the Priscilla bound for Victoria, Australia, on 15 October 1852. [NRS.HD4/5]

BETHUNE, MATTHEW TOWNSEND., MD, born 1791, died in Inverness on 12 April 1823. [Chapel Yard gravestone, Inverness]

BETHUNE, NORMAN, born 1820, Catherine born 1824, born 1824, Finlay born 1830, Janet born 1848, and Ann born 1850, from

Romesdale, Skye, emigrated via Liverpool aboard the Priscilla bound for Victoria, Australia, on 15 October 1852. [NRS.HD4/5]

BETHUNE, PETER, born 1830, from Uig, Skye, emigrated via Liverpool aboard the Priscilla bound for Victoria, Australia, on 15 October 1852. [NRS.HD4/5]

BEVERLY, GEORGE, a vintner in Inverness, testament, 8 January 1790, Comm. Inverness. [NRS]

BIRNIE, WILLIAM, a merchant in Inverness, 1814. [NRS.S36.9.71]

BLACK, JAMES, in Fort William, sequestration, 1806. [NRS.CS234.B2.1]

BLACK, JAMES, from Inverness, settled in Canada de la Janive near Bodega Bay, California, in the 1820s. [SHR.153/141]

BLACK, ROBERT, born 1784, a plumber in Inverness, died on 12 July 1851, husband of Harriet Loughton born 1790, died 9 April 1848. [Chapel Yard gravestone, Inverness]

BLAIR, DAVID, born 20 March 1733 in Inverness, a merchant who died in St John, New Brunswick, on 2 October 1798. [St John Gazette, 2.10.1798]

BLAIR, PETER, born 1766 in Inverness-shire, a merchant in St John, New Brunswick, died 16 August 1808, administration, 1808, New Brunswick.

BOLMAN, Mrs JANE, born in Lochaber, wife of Dr John Bolman, died in Lunenburg, Nova Scotia, on 3 March 1829. [AR, 14.3.1829]

BOYD, ALEXANDER, a labourer from Arisaig, [Arasaig], emigrated via Fort William aboard the Dove of Aberdeen bound for Pictou, Nova Scotia, in 1801. [NRS.RH2.4.87, 73-5]

BOYD, ALEXANDER, a labourer in Arisaig, [Aragaig], Mary Boyd a spinner, emigrated via Fort William on board the Dove of Aberdeen bound for Pictou, Nova Scotia, in 1801. [NRS.RH2.4.87.75-5]

BOYD, ANGUS, a labourer in Arisaig, [Arasaig], John Boyd born 1794, emigrated via Fort William on board the Dove of Aberdeen bound for Pictou, Nova Scotia, in 1801. [NRS.RH2.4.87.75-5]

BOYD, ANNE, a spinner in Arisaig, [Arasaig], emigrated via Fort William on board the Dove of Aberdeen bound for Pictou, Nova Scotia, in 1801. [NRS.RH2.4.87.75-5]

BOYD, HUGH, a labourer in Arisaig, [Arasaig], Mary Boyd a spinner, Bell MacFarlane born 1789, Mary Boyd born 1797, emigrated via Fort William on board the Dove of Aberdeen bound for Pictou, Nova Scotia, in 1801. [NRS.RH2.4.87.75-5]

BOYD, JOHN, a tenant in Arisaig, [Arasaig], Catherine Boyd a spinner, emigrated via Fort William on board the Dove of Aberdeen bound for Pictou, Nova Scotia, in 1801. [NRS.RH2.4.87.75-5]

BOYNE, JEREMIAH COGHLAN, from Inverness, graduated MA from King's College, Aberdeen, in March 1845, later in Bengal. [KCA]

BRANDER, JAMES S., born 31 December 1795 in Inverness, emigrated to USA in 1810, married Harriet A. McCulloch in Petersburg, Virginia, in 1820, a merchant in New York, New Orleans, and Virginia, also a shipowner, and marine insurance broker, died in New York on 13 February 1876. [ANY]

BREMNER, ARCHIBALD, born 1806, for 33 years master of Raining School, Inverness, died 6 July 1866, husband of Isabella Calder, born 1818, died 29 April 1841, parents of Isabella Calder Bremner who died in Lahore, India, on 1 April 1885. [Chapel Yard gravestone, Inverness]

BREWSTER, Sir DAVID, of Belleville House, Kingussie, letters, 1833-1834. [NRS.GD46.1.68]

BROWN, Mrs ANNE, from Inverness, now in the USA, widow of William Benjamin Brown a shipmaster in Charleston, South Carolina, 1828. [NRS.CS17.1.4/101]

BROWN, JAMES, born 1806, a gunner at Fort George, was accused of culpable homicide in 1838. [NRS.AD14.38.5]

BROWN, JOHN, an officer of the Revenue, who was obstructed at Strone, Kingussie, in 1823. [NRS.JC26.1823.12]

BRUCE, ALEXANDER, born 1836, son of James Bruce, [1792-1864], and his wife Janet McDonald, [1805-1876], died in Jamaica in September 1864. [Tomnacross gravestone]

BRUCE, ANN, born 1836, from Uig, emigrated via Liverpool aboard the Priscilla bound for Victoria, Australia, on 15 October 1852. [NRS.HD4/5]

BUCHANAN, ALEXANDER, born 1814, wife Catherine born 1814, daughter Mary born 1835, son John born 1837, son Malcolm born 1841, daughter Kate born 1846, and Christy born 1852, from Borneskitaig, Skye, emigrated via Liverpool aboard the Priscilla bound for Victoria, Australia, on 15 October 1852. [NRS.HD4/5]

BUCHANAN, ARTHUR, born 1751, barrack-master of Fort Augustus, died on 24 January 1821. [Kilchuimen gravestone]

BUCHANAN, CATHERINE, born 1808, daughter Flora born 1833, daughter Catherine born BU1838, and daughter Jane born 1840, from Garros, Skye, emigrated via Liverpool aboard the Allison bound for Melbourne, Australia, on 13 September 1852. [NRS.HD4/5]

BUCHANAN, JOHN, born 1823, wife Mary born 1824, son Donald born 1843, and daughter Mary born 1852, from Achnahanait, emigrated via Liverpool aboard the Priscilla bound for Victoria, Australia, on 15 October 1852. [NRS.HD4/5]

BURNETT, ALEXANDER, born 1786, tacksman of Kinchyle and factor for the estate of Ness Castle, died at Culduthel on 22 November 1865, husband of Anne Gillinders, born 1790, died at Culduthel on 12 March 1872. [Dores gravestone]

CALDER, ALEXANDER, from Inverness, graduated MA from King's College, Aberdeen, on 30 March 1807. [KCA]

CALDER, DUNCAN, born 1765 in Inverness-shire, died at Meagher's Grant, Nova Scotia, on 18 May 1841. [HJ:15.4.1841]

CALDER, JAMES, from Inverness, graduated MA from King's College, Aberdeen, on 29 March 1805. [KCA]

CALDER, PATRICK, from Inverness, a student in Marischal College, Aberdeen, around 1800. [MCA]

CALLUM, WILLIAM, born 1793 in Kiltarlity, husband of Catherine born 1809 in Dingwall, formerly a sawyer now a pauper in Duff Street, Inverness, in 1857. [IPR]

CAMERON, ALEXANDER, born 1727 in Glenmoriston, emigrated to America in 1773, settled on the Kingsborough Patent, New York, a Loyalist soldier of the Royal Regiment of New York from 1780 to 1783, relocated to Cornwall, Ontario, died in January 1823. [DFpp]

CAMERON, ALEXANDER, [1767-1857], and his wife Anne...... [1777-1853] in Munerrigie, Glengarry, parents of Ewen Cameron who settled in Australia before 1854. [Gairlochy gravestone]

CAMERON, ALEXANDER, tacksman of Auchnanellen, father of Kitty Cameron wife of John Cameron in Caledonia, Genesee County, New York, in 1813. [NRS.CS17.1.33/49]

CAMERON, ALEXANDER, a farmer from Urquhart, with Helen, Alexander a labourer, Ann [born 1788], Flory [born 1794], Mary [born 1798], emigrated via Fort William aboard the Sarah of Liverpool bound for Pictou, Nova Scotia, in June 1801. [NRS.RH2.4.87]

CAMERON, ALEXANDER, with his wife, from Ardnabie, emigrated via Fort William aboard the Friends of Saltcoats master John How to Montreal in July 1802. [GkAd.59]

CAMERON, ALEXANDER, his wife and two children, from Laddy, emigrated via Fort William aboard the Friends of Saltcoats master John How to Montreal in July 1802. [GkAd.59]

CAMERON, ALEXANDER, from Lochielhead, emigrated via Fort William aboard the Friends of Saltcoats master John How to Montreal in July 1802. [GkAd.59]

CAMERON, ALEXANDER, from Inverness, graduated MA from King's College, Aberdeen, on25 March 1814, later Rector of Tain Academy, and minister at Eddertoun. [KCA]

CAMERON, ALEXANDER, born 1802, Free Church schoolmaster in Petty for 36 years and a Sunday school teacher there, died 2 March 1893, husband of Annie McLeod, born 1809, died 4 February 1892. [Brachlich gravestone]

CAMERON, ALEXANDER, a weaver in Strathglass, Kiltarlity, was accused of theft in 1841. [NRS.AD14.41.152]

CAMERON, ALLAN, jr., a merchant in Fort William, accused of fire-raising, was outlawed in 1807. [NRS.JC11.48]

CAMERON, ALLAN, of Clunes, a petition in 1820. [NRS.CC2.7.68.1]

CAMERON, Major ANGUS, born 1761, late of Kinlochleven, died in Seymour, Upper Canada, on 23 August 1847. [AJ.5203][EEC.21556]

CAMERON, ANGUS, [1816-1878], and his wife Elizabeth McDonald, [1817-1878], parents of Janet Kneath Cameron, born 1855, died in Townsville, Australia, in 1897. [Glen Nevis gravestone]

CAMERON, ANNE, born 1815, died 17 November 1887. [Chapel Yard gravestone, Inverness]

CAMERON, ANNE, in Fort William, versus Anne Reid, spouse of Joseph Wilson a vintner in Fort William, in 1800. [NRS.CC2.2.100.4]

CAMERON, ANNE, from Muick, emigrated via Fort William aboard the Friends of Saltcoats master John How to Montreal, Quebec, in July 1802. [GkAd.59]

CAMERON, ARCHIBALD, born 1811, a farm servant in Craigscorry, Kilmorack, was accused of culpable homicide in 1831. [NRS.AD14.31.36]

CAMERON, CATHERINE, Mary Cameron, Marjery Cameron, and two children, from Leck, emigrated via Fort William aboard the Friends of Saltcoats master John How to Montreal in July 1802. [GkAd.59]

CAMERON, CATHERINE, wife of John McDonald, was accused of assaulting Kenneth McLennon from Fort William and Robert Urquhart from Fort Augustus, Revenue Officers, in Boleskine and Abertarff, in 1823, was outlawed. [NRS.JC26.1823.14]

CAMERON, CHARLES, born 16 May 1783 in Inverness, married Sarah Houghton in Toronto, Ontario, in 1808, died in Ontario, on 1 August 1867. [HFHS]

CAMERON, CHRISTINA, eldest daughter of Alexander Cameron in Inverguseran, Inverness-shire, married Reverend Donald McKenzie of the Scots Church at Zorra, London district, at Energiser near St Thomas, Upper Canada, on 28 November 1838. [AJ.4751][SG.735]

CAMERON, COLIN, born 1801, an innkeeper in Letterfinlay, Kilmonivaig, guilty of assault in 1836. [NRS.AD14.36.43]

CAMERON, DANIEL, born 1821, a coach guard in Inverness, died 1 November 1889. [Chapel Yard gravestone, Inverness]

CAMERON, DONALD, and his wife, from Drimsallie, [Druim na Saille], emigrated via Fort William aboard the Friends of Saltcoats master John How to Montreal in July 1802. [GkAd.59]

CAMERON, DONALD, wife and two children, from Kinlocharkaig, emigrated via Fort William aboard the Friends of Saltcoats master John How to Montreal in July 1802. [GkAd.59]

CAMERON, Captain DONALD, from Kinlochiel, settled at La Chine, Montreal, Quebec, around 1805. [NRS.GD202.70.12]

CAMERON, DONALD, in Corrycholly, Kilmonivaig, a victim of embezzlement in 1830. [AD14.36.248]

CAMERON, DONALD MHOR, from Glen Moyl, his wife Ann McLean, and son Euan Dhu Cameron, died at Point Fortune, Canada, in July 1832. [AJ.4422][GA.4270]

CAMERON, DONALD, born 1827, a house-carpenter in Inverness, died 26 February 1878, husband of Margaret Stewart, born 1832, died 9 December 1906. [Chapel Yard gravestone, Inverness]

CAMERON, DONALD, of Lochiel, died in Toulouse, France, on 14 September 1832. [AJ.4426][FH.557]

CAMERON, Reverend DONALD, in Laggan, a sequestration petition in 1846. [NRS.CS279.377]

CAMERON, DUGALD, from Corpach, Fort William, applied to emigrate to Canada in 1818. [TNA.CO384.3]

CAMERON, DUGALD, and his wife Catherine McMaillan, [1804-1843], in Camghail, parents of John Cameron who settled at Portland Bay, Australia. [Kilmallie gravestone]

CAMERON, DUGALD, in Unachan, Kilmonivaig, a victim of assault in 1837. [NRS.AD14.37.1; JC26.1837.70]

CAMERON, DUNCAN, born 1764 in Glenmoriston, son of Alexander Cameron and his wife Margaret McDonell, married Margaret McLeod of Hamer around 1821, settled in Williamstown, Glengarry, Upper Canada. [TML]

CAMERON, DUNCAN, a merchant in Fort William, sequestration of estate, 1810. [NRS.CS36.1.67]

CAMERON, EWEN, a farmer at Kinlochmorar, [Caen Loch Mhorair], emigrated via Fort William on board the Dove of Aberdeen bound for Pictou, Nova Scotia, in 1801. [NRS.RH2.4.87.75-5]

CAMERON, EWAN, son of Donald Cameron [died 1877] and his wife Margaret McLean [died 1850], settled in Australia, [St Finnan's, Arisaig and Moidart gravestone]

CAMERON, JAMES, a labourer at Kinlochmorar, [Caen Loch Mhorair], emigrated via Fort William on board the Dove of Aberdeen bound for Pictou, Nova Scotia, in 1801. [NRS.RH2.4.87.75-5]

CAMERON, JAMES, a slater in Inverness, dead by 1857, father of James Cameron a commission agent in Detroit. [NRS.S/H]; James Cameron, born 1781, a slater and builder in Inverness for over 40 years, died on 10 March 1854, husband of Margaret McDonald, born 1804, died 20 April 1886. [Chapel Yard gravestone, Inverness]

CAMERON, JEAN, born 1780 on Rhum, emigrated via Leith on the St Lawrence of Newcastle bound for Port Hawkesby, Cape Breton, in 1828. [PANS.M6-100]

CAMERON, JEAN, born 1827, widow of James MacMillan in West Chester, New York, died in Inverness on 14 July 1877. [Chapel Yard gravestone, Inverness]

CAMERON, JOHN, his wife, John Cameron, Donald Cameron, Ewen Cameron, from Kenmore, [Cheann Mhor], emigrated via Fort William aboard the Friends of Saltcoats master John How, to Montreal in July 1802. [GkAd.59]

CAMERON, JOHN, with his wife, and Duncan Cameron, from Achnacarry, [Achadh na Cairidh], emigrated via Fort William aboard the Friends of Saltcoats master John How to Montreal in July 1802. [GkAd.59]

CAMERON, JOHN, his brother Angus Cameron, from Glenturret, [Gleann Turraid], emigrated via Fort William aboard the Friends of Saltcoats master John How, to Montreal in July 1802. [GkAd.59]

CAMERON, JOHN, from Inverness, graduated MA from King's College, Aberdeen, in March 1818, later minister at Stornaway and at Eddertoun. [KCA]

CAMERON, Lieutenant Colonel JOHN, of Auchensaul, deceased, an inventory, 1820. [NRS.CC2.7.68.1]

CAMERON, JOHN, in Corrycholly, Kilmonivaig, a victim of embezzlement in 1830. [AD14.36.248]

CAMERON, JOHN, born 1794 in Inverness, died in Farm, Jamaica, on 13 September 1835. [AJ.4596]

CAMERON, JOHN, born in Campbellton, Ardesier, in 1793, died 26 August 1858. [Brachlich gravestone]

CAMERON, JOHN, born 1809, son of Donald Roy Cameron, tenant in Ratlichmore, Kilmonivaig, guilty of assault in 1836. [NRS.AD14.36.43; JC26.1836.109]

CAMERON, JOHN, in Blair Macvoillich, was accused of sheep stealing, outlawed in 1817. [NRS.JC11.58]

CAMERON, JOHN, tacksman of Knockfin, Beauly, trial, 1837. [NRS.JC11.84]

CAMERON, JOHN, of Glen Nevis, then in Berbice, a sasine, 1850. [NRS.RS38.PR54.276]

CAMERON, LEWIS, born 1822, a hotel keeper in Inverness, died 1 May 1856. [Chapel Yard gravestone, Inverness]

CAMERON, MARTIN, son of Donald Cameron [died 1877] and his wife Margaret McLean [died 1850], settled in Australia, [St Finnan's, Arisaig and Moidart gravestone]

CAMERON, MURDOCH, born 1775, a butcher in Inverness, died 27 September 1834, husband of Katherine McMaster, born 1787, died 30 September 1834, parents of Donald Cameron, born 1801, a coachman in Dochfour, died 30 April 1881, his wife Margaret Shaw, born 1801, died 6 May 1882, and daughter Amelia Cameron, born 1834, died 27 January 1905. [Chapel Yard gravestone, Inverness]

CAMERON, PATRICK, of Glen Nevis, a petition in 1820. [NRS.CC2.7.68.1]

CAMERON, RODERICK, a labourer at Kinlochmorar, [Ceann Loch Mhorar], Eliza born 1787, Mary born 1797, Margaret born 1798, and Christian born 1799, emigrated via Fort William on board the Dove of Aberdeen bound for Pictou, Nova Scotia, in 1801. [NRS.RH2.4.87.75-5]

CAMERON, SARAH, second daughter of D. Cameron from Inverness-shire, married Robert Dey from Dufftown, Banffshire, in New York on 3 April 1873. [EC.27629]

CAMERON, Mrs, widow of Donald Cameron of the family of Lochiel, died in New Providence, Bahamas, in 1806. [DPCA.204]

CAMPBELL, ALEXANDER, from Inverness, graduated MA from King's College, Aberdeen, on 2 April 1804, later a master of Inverness Academy, and minister at Dores and Croy. [KCA][F.6.451]

CAMPBELL, ALEXANDER, in Achnacroish, Kilmonivaig, letters to Sir Duncan Campbell of Barcaldine between 1814 and 1822. [NRS.GD170.2274]

CAMPBELL, Reverend ALEXANDER, a victim of the riot at Croy Church in 1823. [NRS.AD14.23.35]

CAMPBELL, ALEXANDER, innkeeper in the Kirkton of Glenelg, was accused of stealing goats in 1837. [NRS.AD14.37.18]

CAMPBELL, ANGUS, from Inverness-shire, married Margaret Grant, youngest daughter of Peter Grant, in Halifax, Nova Scotia, on 17 June 1838. [Acadian Recorder.23.6.1838]

CAMPBELL, COLIN, sheriff substitute at Fort William in a letter to Sir James Grant writes – "Two vessels have left for Nova Scotia with emigrants, the Dove of Aberdeen, bound for Pictou, with 219 souls and sundry provisions; it was agreed that provisions were adequate for ten weeks, but that the passengers were too crowded and 20 full passengers have been removed to the Sarah of Liverpool, containing 350 souls; stores have been provided for the passengers from Liverpool and by the exertions of the Roman Catholic clergy and other inhabitants of Fort William; Mr Denoon travelled in the Sarah and has acted very fairly; a list of the emigrants to be laid before the Lord Advocate; writer spoke personally to them all; 'it was in vain to tell them of the visionary and hazardous plan they had adopted nor did Mr Denoon appear to me to encourage them with any Ideal prospects on landing', dated 26 June 1801". [NRS.GD248.671.6]

CAMPBELL, COLIN COILLAIN, a master mariner in New York, nephew and heir of Farquhar McIvar, minister in Glenshiel, who died on 20 September 1863. [NRS.S/H]

CAMPBELL, DONALD, tenant on Canna, 1818. [C.220]

CAMPBELL, DONALD, a tenant on Canna in 1851. [C.299]

CAMPBELL, DUNCAN, from Inverness, graduated MA from King's College, Aberdeen, in March 1825, later minister at Berrow. [KCA]

CAMPBELL, JANE URQUHART ROY, born 1814, wife of Major Robert Watson of the Ceylon Rifle Regiment, died in Inverness on 8 January 1856. [Kirkton of Ardersier gravestone]

CAMPBELL, JOHN, Lieutenant Governor of Fort George, testament, 10 July 1798, Comm. Inverness. [NRS]

CAMPBELL, JOHN, of Glen More, a petition in 1820. [NRS.CC2.7.68.1]

CAMPBELL, LOUISA, widow of Lieutenant Colonel John Cameron of Auchansaul, in Fort William, a petition in 1820. [NRS.CC2.7.68.1]

CAMPBELL, JOHN, from Inverness, graduated MA from King's College, Aberdeen, in March 1826. [KCA]

CAMPBELL, MALCOLM, with the widow Campbell, tenants on Canna, 1818. [C.220]

CAMPBELL, PATRICK, from Inverness, graduated MA from King's College, Aberdeen, in March 1832, later minister at Killearnan. [KCA]

CAMPBELL, PRYCE JOHN, son of Alexander Campbell the Sheriff Substitute of Inverness, died in the West Indies in 1795. [SM.57.749]

CAMPBELL, ROBERT, of Sonachan, letters to Sir Duncan Campbell of Barcaldine between 1828 and 1833. [NRS.GD170.2366]

CAMPBELL, Lieutenant RUPERT, bon 1784, late of the 78th Highlanders and of the Ceylon Rifle Regiment, died at Reay Bank, Ardersier, on 17 July 1861. [Kirkton of Ardersier gravestone]

CAMPBELL, SARAH, born 1808 in Glenelg, wife of Laughlin Sinclair, died in Campbeltown, New Brunswick, on 3 July 1843. [Gleaner and Northumberland Schediasma, 4.8.1843]

CAMPBELL, WALLACE, born 1803 in Inverness, was drowned at Carleton, New Brunswick, on 31 October 1835. [NBC.7.11.1835]

CAMPBELL, Major WILLIAM, of the 78th Regiment of Foot, appointed John Hutcheson Fraser in Wester Lovat, Kirkhill, as his factor in 1806. [NRS.GD23.10.655]

CAMPBELL, WILLIAM, from Inverness, graduated MA from King's College, Aberdeen, in March 1818, later minister of Coull. [KCA]

CAMPBELL, WILLIAM, from Skye, emigrated via Greenock aboard the Royal Adelaide bound for St John, New Brunswick, later to Fredericton, petitioned the New Brunswick House of Assembly in 1838. [PANB.RS24/4/77]

CARGILL, JAMES, son of John Cargill in Inverness, a student at Marischal College, Aberdeen, around 1820. [MCA]

CARRICK, R., in Fort Augustus, a letter to James Grant clerk of the peace in Inverness in 1804. [NRS.GD23.6.409]

CATTENACH, JOHN, born 1760 in Inverness-shire, late a Captain of the 92nd Highlanders, fought in the Peninsular War, died in Woodhouse, Upper Canada, on 18 August 1852. [W.XIII.1368] [S.25.9.1852]

CHAPMAN, JOSEPH, born 1770, clerk of works at Fort George, died 9 May 1834, husband of Mary Stirling. [Kirkton of Ardersier gravestone]

CHISHOLM, ALEXANDER, of Chisholm, testament, 10 April 1794. [NRS]

CHISHOLM, ALEXANDER, a merchant in Inverness, testament, 26 February 1800, Comm. Inverness. [NRS]

CHISHOLM, ALEXANDER, born 1738 in Inverness, son of John Ban Chisholm and his wife Catherine MacRae, settled in South Carolina around 1746, a planter in South Carolina and in Georgia, died on 10 December 1810. [Old Scots gravestone, Charleston]

CHISHOLM, ALEXANDER, son of William Chisholm the Provost of Inverness, [Inbhir Nis], died on Friendship Plantation, Demerara, on 16 July 1799. [GC.1190][EA]

CHISHOLM, ALEXANDER, a farmer from Strathglass, with Mary, emigrated via Fort William aboard the Sarah of Liverpool bound for Pictou, Nova Scotia, in June 1801. [NRS.RH2.4.87]

CHISHOLM, ALEXANDER, a labourer from Strathglass, with Margaret, and Margaret, emigrated via Fort William aboard the Sarah of Liverpool bound for Pictou, Nova Scotia, in June 1801. [NRS.RH2.4.87]

CHISHOLM, ALEXANDER, a farmer from Strathglass, with Mary, Duncan [born 1787], Catherine [born 1794], Catherine [born 1797], and Patrick [born 1798], emigrated via Fort William aboard the Sarah of Liverpool bound for Pictou, Nova Scotia, in June 1801. [NRS.RH2.4.87]

CHISHOLM, ALEXANDER, a farmer from Kilmorack, with Helen, Catherine, Margaret [born q787], Ann [born 1789], Alexander [born 1791], Helen [born 1793], Isobel [born 1795], Colin [born 1799], and an infant, emigrated via Fort William aboard the Sarah of Liverpool bound for Pictou, Nova Scotia, in June 1801. [NRS.RH2.4.87]

CHISHOLM, ALPIN, [1830-1912], and his wife Catherine McDonald, [1830-1891], parents of Alpin Chisholm who settled in Morris, Manitoba.

CHISHOLM, ANNE, and Mary Chisholm, from Strathglass, emigrated via Fort William aboard the Friends of Saltcoats master John How, to

Montreal in July 1802, Ann died in Antigonish, Nova Scotia, in 1832. [GkAd.59][CMM][IC.28.3.1832]

CHISHOLM, ARCHIBALD, a farmer from Kilmorack, with Catherine, Isobel, Ann, and Catherine [born 1789], emigrated via Fort William aboard the Sarah of Liverpool bound for Pictou, Nova Scotia, in June 1801. [NRS.RH2.4.87]

CHISHOLM, ARCHIBALD, a farmer from Kilmorack, emigrated via Fort William aboard the Sarah of Liverpool bound for Pictou, Nova Scotia, in June 1801. [NRS.RH2.4.87]

CHISHOLM, ARCHIBALD, a tenant in Kilmorack, with Ann, and an infant, emigrated via Fort William aboard the Sarah of Liverpool bound for Pictou, Nova Scotia, in June 1801. [NRS.RH2.4.87]

CHISHOLM, ARCHIBALD, a labourer from Kiltarlity, emigrated via Fort William aboard the Sarah of Liverpool bound for Pictou, Nova Scotia, in June 1801. [NRS.RH2.4.87]

CHISHOLM, ARCHIBALD, was found guilty of housebreaking and theft in Inverness in 1813, was sentenced to transportation to the colonies for 7 years. [NRS.GD1.959]

CHISHOLM, ARCHIBALD, jr., in Strathglass, was accused of housebreaking and theft in 1814, charge not proven in court. [NRS.JC26.1814.10]

CHISHOLM, CATHERINE, born 1730 in Inverness, died in Douglas, Nova Scotia, on 2 January 1828. [Acadian Recorder, 19.1.1828]

CHISHOLM, CATHERINE, daughter of Captain H. Chisholm latterly Fort Major of Fort Augustus, Inverness-shire, married Ira Mosher in St John, New Brunswick, on 16 June 1841. [NBC.3.7.1841]

CHISHOLM, COLIN, from Inverness, graduated MD from King's College, Aberdeen, in 1793, later a physician in Grenada. [KCA]

CHISHOLM, COLIN, a labourer from Kiltarlity, emigrated via Fort William aboard the Sarah of Liverpool bound for Pictou, Nova Scotia, in June 1801. [NRS.RH2.4.87]

CHISHOLM, COLIN, a solicitor in Inverness, 1836. [NRS.CS46.1836.7.156]

CHISHOLM, DONALD OG, born 1756 in Clachan, Strathglass, died in Nova Scotia on 29 February 1840. [Nova Scotian, 4.3.1840]

CHISHOLM, DONALD, born 1797 in Inverness, son of Alexander Chisholm a merchant and his wife Mary Robertson, graduated MA from King's College, Aberdeen, in March 1818, later minister at Boleskine and Abertarff from 1840 until his death on 2 August 1857. [KCA]F.6.446]

CHISHOLM, DONALD, born 1853, died in Delnorte, Colorado, on 24 March 1917. [Clachan Comair gravestone, Inverness-shire]

CHISHOLM, DUNCAN, a farmer from Kilmorack, with Ann and an infant, emigrated via Fort William aboard the Sarah of Liverpool bound for Pictou, Nova Scotia, in June 1801. [NRS.RH2.4.87]

CHISHOLM, DUNCAN, a labourer from Kilmorack, with Ann, emigrated via Fort William aboard the Sarah of Liverpool bound for Pictou, Nova Scotia, in June 1801. [NRS.RH2.4.87]

CHISHOLM, EMILIA C., relict of William Mackintosh of Baliaspick, was granted a tack of shooting rights at Dunachton by The Mackintosh in 1821. [NRS.GD176.1453]

CHISHOLM, HAROLD, born 1792, late of the 92nd Highlanders, died on 19 September 1855, husband of Janet Cameron, born 1802, died 4 March 1858. [Old High gravestone, Inverness]

CHISHOLM, HUGH FRASER, born 1815 in Inverness, died on 27 August 1843 in Nappan, Nova Scotia. [New Brunswick Courier.2.9.1843]

CHISHOLM, JAMES, a farmer from Urquhart, with Martha, Isabel [born 1787], Mary [born 1789], James [born 1791], Catherine [born 1794], John [born 1796], Ewan [born 1799], emigrated via Fort William aboard the Sarah of Liverpool bound for Pictou, Nova Scotia, in June 1801. [NRS.RH2.4.87]

CHISHOLM, JAMES FRASER, born 1799, eldest son of Captain Hugh Fraser in Fort Augustus, died on Plantation Helena, Demerara, on 26 September 1822. [SM.91.127]

CHISHOLM, JANET, from Kilmorack, emigrated via Fort William aboard the Sarah of Liverpool bound for Pictou, Nova Scotia, in June 1801. [NRS.RH2.4.87]

CHISHOLM, JANET, born 1790 in Mauld, Kiltarlity, an outside labourer and a pauper in 10 Gilbert Street, Inverness, in 1857. [IPR]

CHISHOLM, JOHN, a labourer from Kiltarlity, with Flora, emigrated via Fort William aboard the Sarah of Liverpool bound for Pictou, Nova Scotia, in June 1801. [NRS.RH2.4.87]

CHISHOLM, JOHN, a farmer from Strathglass, with Ann, John [born 1792], Alexander [born 1794], Colin [born 1796], David [born 1799], emigrated via Fort William aboard the Sarah of Liverpool bound for Pictou, Nova Scotia, in June 1801. [NRS.RH2.4.87]

CHISHOLM, JOHN, born 1786, from Strathglass, emigrated via Fort William aboard the Sarah of Liverpool bound for Pictou, Nova Scotia, in June 1801. [NRS.RH2.4.87]

CHISHOLM, JOHN, a farmer from Kilmorack, with Catherine, Donald a labourer, Colin a labourer, William a labourer, and Margaret, [born 1789], emigrated via Fort William aboard the Sarah of Liverpool bound for Pictou, Nova Scotia, in June 1801. [NRS.RH2.4.87]

23

CHISHOLM, JOHN, a farmer from Kilmorack, emigrated via Fort William aboard the Sarah of Liverpool bound for Pictou, Nova Scotia, in June 1801. [NRS.RH2.4.87]

CHISHOLM, KENNETH, in Comar, Strathglass, was accused of assaulting a Revenue Officer, was outlawed in 1825. [NRS.JC26.1825.68]

CHISHOLM, LEWIS, born 1770 in Inverness-shire, died in Montreal on 26 June 1847, his wife Hannah McDonald, born 1773, died on 8 July 1847. [AJ.5197]

CHISHOLM, MARGARET, from Kilmorack, emigrated via Fort William aboard the Sarah of Liverpool bound for Pictou, Nova Scotia, in June 1801. [NRS.RH2.4.87]

CHISHOLM, MARY, born 1796 in Glen Urquhart, a spinner in Sconce Factory later, a pauper in Tomnahurich Street, Inverness, in 1857. [IPR]

CHISHOLM, RODERICK, a farmer from Kilmorack, emigrated via Fort William aboard the Sarah of Liverpool bound for Pictou, Nova Scotia, in June 1801. [NRS.RH2.4.87]

CHISHOLM, RORY, tenant in Strathglass, with Mary, Mary, and Christian [born 1789], emigrated via Fort William aboard the Sarah of Liverpool bound for Pictou, Nova Scotia, in June 1801. [NRS.RH2.4.87]

CHISHOLM, WILLIAM, a farmer from Kilmorack, with Mary, Alexander a labourer, Donald a labourer, Margaret, Catherine [born 1787], Kenneth [born 1793], William [born 1797], Colin [born 1798], and an infant, emigrated via Fort William aboard the Sarah of Liverpool bound for Pictou, Nova Scotia, in June 1801. [NRS.RH2.4.87]

CHISHOLM, WILLIAM, a tailor from Strathglass, with Catherine, Catherine [born 1792], Anne [born 1797], Alexander [born 1798] emigrated via Fort William aboard the <u>Sarah of Liverpool</u> bound for Pictou, Nova Scotia, in June 1801. [NRS.RH2.4.87]

CHISHOLM. Reverend WILLIAM, from Inverness-shire, died 31 August 1819. [Antigonish gravestone, NS]

CLARK, ALEXANDER, born 1797 in Inverness, graduated MA from King's College, Aberdeen, in 1813, a schoolmaster in Alves, ordained in 1822, minister in Inverness, from 1822 until his death on 6 May 1852. [F.6.459]

CLARK, ALEXANDER, a merchant in Inverness, 1812. [NRS.CS36.7.20]

CLARK, ALEXANDER, late Ordnance Barrack master in Athlone, Ireland, died in Inverness on 4 October 1822, husband of Elizabeth Burnes. [Kirkton of Bunchrew gravestone]

CLARK, DANIEL, from Inverness, graduated MA from King's College, Aberdeen, in March 1822, later a minister in Minch, Canada. [KCA]

CLARK, GEORGE, born 1833, son of William Clark and his wife Elizabeth Fraser, died in Camp Savanna, Jamaica, on 21 May 1858. [Chapel Yard gravestone, Inverness]

CLARK, or FRASER, ISABELLA, born 1806 in Kirkhill, a domestic servant now a pauper in Torbreck in 1857, mother of several children including William born 1835 now in Australia. [IPR]

CLARK, JAMES, master of the <u>Newburgh of Inverness</u> trading with Fort William in 1806. [NRS.E504.17.8]

CLARK, JOHN, born 1758 in Petty, [Peitidh], emigrated to South Carolina, a teacher there and in Georgia, later a Baptist missionary in Georgia from 1789 until 1833, died in St Louis, Missouri, in 1833. [TSA]

CLARK, JOHN, from Inverness, graduated MA from King's College, Aberdeen, on 28 March 1801, later master of Inverness Academy. [KCA]

CLARK, JOHN, a planter in Demerara, died in 1809, testament, 1811, Comm. Edinburgh. [NRS]

CLARK, JOHN, with his wife Mary Grant, and their eight children, from Tomfad, Fhearnasdail, Glen Feshie, Inverness-shire, emigrated in 1833 to Puslinch, Upper Canada, [HS.16.4.17]

CLARK, JOHN, born 1782, a merchant in Inverness, died 28 August 1857, husband of Katherine McKenzie, born 1791, died 6 February 1860. [Chapel Yard gravestone, Inverness]

CLARKE, KENNETH, died in New Westminster, British Columbia, on 28 September 1886, son of John Clarke [1805-1875] and his wife Margaret McLennan, [1802-1881]. [Brachlich gravestone]

CLARK, MARGARET, born 1815, died 13 February 1861, wife of Donald Noble a pawnbroker in Inverness. [Chapel Yard gravestone, Inverness]

CLARK, MARY B., eldest daughter of Robert Clark a surgeon at Fort Augustus, married Alexander Stewart McLennan, in Montreal, Quebec, on 1 October 1859. [CM.21869]

CLARK, WILLIAM, with his wife and nine children, from Fhearnasdail, Glen Feshie, Inverness-shire, emigrated in 1833 to Puslinch, Upper Canada, [HS.16.4.17]

CLUNAS, ALLAN, from Glen Pean, settled at La Chine, Montreal, Quebec, around 1805. [NRS.GD202.70.12]

CLUNAS, CATHARINE ANN, born 1839, wife of Evander McIver an architect, died in Brunswick, Melbourne, Australia, on 8 June 1874. [Chapel Yard gravestone, Inverness]

CLUNAS, JAMES, born 1809, son of William Clunas and his wife Janet McKay, formerly in New Orleans, Louisiana, died in Nairn on 2 January 1888. [Wardlaw gravestone, Inverness]

CLUNAS, WILLIAM, born 1787, died 12 April 1861, husband of Elizabeth McKenzie, born 1801, died 13 April 1868, parents of John Clunas, born 1839, late of Mount Cole, Australia, died in Inverness on 3 December 1903. [Chapel Yard gravestone, Inverness]

COBBAN, HUGH, a merchant in Inverness, 1814. [NRS.CS36.11.104]

COCHRANE, Major THOMAS, in Fort William, 1808. [NRS.CS228B.14.46]

COLLINS, Mrs HECTORINA, born in Inverness, wife of ..... Collins a merchant in Georgetown, Demerara, died on Plantation Amsterdam, Demerara, on 25 February 1844. [AJ.5024]

COLVIN, DUNCAN, was granted a tack of Essick, for nineteen years in 1840. [NRS.GD176.1453]

COLVIN, JOHN, in Torbreck, a deposition re Alexander Mackintosh of Mackintosh in 1820. [NRS.GD176.902]

COOPER, ELIZABETH, daughter of John Cooper in St Kitts, married Dr Chisholm from Grenada, in Inverness on 22 December 1794. [EA.3235.422]

CORBET, JOHN, with his wife, William Corbet, Christy Corbet, and one child, from Ardachy, [Ardachaidh], emigrated via Fort William aboard the Friends of Saltcoats master John How to Montreal, Quebec, in July 1802. [GkAd.59]

CORBET, KENNETH, in Inverness, graduated MD from King's College, Aberdeen, on 13 April 1854. [KCA]

CORMICK, ALEXANDER, born 1782, the Collector of Excise in Inverness, died 18 January 1855, husband of Elizabeth Corbett, born 1781, died 16 October 1864, parents of Isabella Cormick, born 1820, died 14 April 1897. [Chapel Yard gravestone, Inverness]

CORMACK, DONALD, master of the Inverness of Inverness trading with Easdale in 1805. [NRS.E504.17.8]

COWAN, JAMES, born 1811, died in Inverness on 5 September 1856, his wife, Agnes Adam, born 1808, died at Beaufort Villa, on 17 November 1893. [Chapel Yard gravestone, Inverness]

COWIE, ANDREW, born 1828, son of Andrew Cowie, [1793-1857], and his wife Marjory McDonald, [1797-1883], died in New Orleans in September 1854. [Chapel Yard gravestone, Inverness]

CRUICKSHANK, WILLIAM, born 1812, for 36 years tacksman of Milton of Brachlich, parish of Petty, died 17 April 1879, husband of Barbara Rose, born 1833, died in Reaybank, Ardesier, on 24 January 1923. [Brachlich gravestone]

CUMMING, ALEXANDER, in Grishernich, Duirinish, victim of sheep stealing in 1837. [NRS.AD14.37.4]

CUMMINGS, ALEXANDER, born 1762 in Inverness, died 20 November 1847. [Anglican cemetery, Halifax County, NS]

CUMMING, EWEN, born 1808 in Urquhart and Glen Moriston, a tailor and a pauper in Castle Street, Inverness, in 1857, father of Jess born 1835 now in Australia, etc. [IPR]

CUMMING, LAUCHLAN, Land Surveyor of the Customs at the Port of Inverness in 1821. [NRS.E504.17.9]

CUMING, WILLIAM, a glazier in Inverness, testament, 12 November 1800, Comm. Inverness. [NRS]

CUTHBERT, GEORGE, in Spanish Town, Jamaica, son of Lewis Cuthbert of Bogbain, Inverness, an inventory, 1807. [NRS.GD23.4.243]

CUTHBERT, JANE, widow of Lewis Cuthbert of Castlehill, Inverness, and Jamaica, died in Clifton, Gloucestershire, on 28 September 1830. [GM.100.380]

CUTHBERT, KATHERINE, widow of Jonathan Low a tinplate maker in Aberdeen, testament, 28 April 1791, Comm. Inverness. [NRS]

CUTHBERT, LEWIS, from Castlehill, Inverness, acting Provost Marshal of Jamaica in 1790, settled in St Jago de la Vega, Jamaica, an Assemblyman, died on Clifton Estate, Jamaica, on 28 October 1802. [GM.72.1162][NRS.RS38.GR484.32; RD4.259.1303]

DALLAS, FARQUHAR, a merchant, son of Alexander Dallas a saddler in Inverness, died in Calcutta, India, on 20 June 1840. [AJ.3838]

DALLAS, WILLIAM, born 1788, a baillie of Inverness, died 3 September 1868, husband of Elizabeth Falconer, born 1791, died 14 March 1869. [Chapel Yard gravestone, Inverness]

DAVIDSON, ANDREW, born 1814, died 18 March 1875, husband of Jane Mackay, born 1815, died 12 November 1888. [Chapel Yard gravestone, Inverness]

DAVIDSON, DONALD, born 1789, a shipowner in Inverness, died in September 1849, husband of Ann MacArthur, born 1800, died in January 1860, also her brother John MacArthur, born 1827, died in 1859. [Chapel Yard gravestone, Inverness]

DAVIDSON, DONALD, master of the Peggy of Inverness trading with Dundee in 1821. [NRS.E504.17.8]

DAVIDSON, DONALD, was granted a tack of Altnaslannach, Moy, for twelve years in 1853. [NRS.GD176.1453]

DAVIDSON, ELSPETH, born December 1781, daughter of William Davidson and his wife in Croy, Dalcross, a spinster in Lanniweig, Almy, emigrated to New York aboard the George of New York on 12 August 1807. [TNA.PC1.3790]

DAVIDSON, EWAN, in Kingussie, a sequestration petition in 1846. [NRS.CS278.2.57]

DAVIDSON, JANET, born 1790 in Inverness, a servant and pauper in Haugh in 1857. [IPR]

DAVIDSON, THOMAS, from Inverness, graduated MA from King's College, Aberdeen, in March 1819, later schoolmaster of Dores, then minister of Kilmalie, joined the Free Church. [KCA]

DEAN, DAVID, a merchant in Inverness, testament, 21 January 1799, Comm. Inverness. [NRS]

DENOON, DAVID, born 1759 in Inverness, died in South Carolina on 30 January 1805. [Old Scots gravestone, Charleston]

DENOON, HUGH, born 1746 in Redcastle parish, a judge and Customs Collector at Pictou, Nova Scotia, died at Bellville, Pictou, on 24 March 1836. [New Brunswick Courier, 16.4.1836]

DENOON, JAMES, from Inverness, graduated MA from King's College, Aberdeen, on 29 March 1805, later schoolmaster in Ardesier, then a minister at Dunrossness, Kingarth, and Rothesay. [KCA]

DENOON, JEAN, in Church Street, Inverness, widow of Charles Jamieson a goldsmith there, died in Inverness on 10 May 1838, probate 1838 in Halifax, Nova Scotia.

DIAMOND, DONALD, and Donald Davidson, were granted a tack of Invereen, Strathnairn, for nineteen years in 1839. [NRS.GD176.1453]

DONALD, ALEXANDER, master of the Recovery of Inverness trading with Easdale in 1827. [NRS.E504.17.9]

DONALDSON, Major WILLIAM, born 28 December 1818, sometime of the Scots Guards, later Major of the 2nd Battalion of the Queen's Own Cameron Highlanders, also an Elder of Inverness parish, died on 23 September 1887, husband of Sarah Critchfield, born 1835, died 23 April 1894. [Old High gravestone, Inverness]

DOUGLAS, JOHN, was found guilty of mobbing and rioting and was sentenced at Inverness to transportation to the colonies for 7 years, at Inverness in 1815. [NRS.GD1.959]

DUFF, ALEXANDER ARTHUR, of the Royal Regiment of Foot, born 1800, died at Negapatam, India, on 20 July 1821. [Old High Church, Inverness]

DUFF, HUGH ROBERT, of Muirtown, versus Thomas Alexander Fraser of Lovat, re salmon fishing in the Beauly Firth in 1827. [NRS.GD23.10.719]

DUFF, JANE DOROTHY STRAITON, born 1818, youngest daughter of Hugh Robert Duff in Muirtown, Inverness, wife of Captain R. Shireff, died in Madras, India, on 8 June 1841. [AJ.4884]

DUFF, JOHN, a labourer from Kilmorack, with Catherine, and an infant, emigrated via Fort William aboard the Sarah of Liverpool bound for Pictou, Nova Scotia, in June 1801. [NRS.RH2.4.87]

DUNBAR, WILLIAM, from Inverness, graduated from King's College, Aberdeen, on 26 April 1813, later a minister in Nova Scotia. [KCA]

ELLIOT, SAMUEL M., from Inverness, was naturalised in New York on 12 September 1837. [N.Y. Superior Court Records]

ELLIS, ARCHIBALD, from Inverness, graduated MA from King's College, Aberdeen, on 30 March 1821. [KCA]

ETTLES, ALEXANDER, son of John Ettles and Letitia Lamford, died in Cadiz, Spain, on 29 June 1809. [Chapel Yard gravestone, Inverness]

ETTLES, JOHN, born 1745, died 8 December 1808, husband of Letitia Lamford, born 1752, died 20 February 1838. [Chapel Yard gravestone, Inverness]

ETTLES, JOHN, son of Robert Ettles in Inverness, died in Demerara on 26 July 1823. [EA.5199.271]

EWING, DANIEL, youngest son of Thomas Ewing in Keppoch, [A Cheapach], died in Charleston, South Carolina, on 23 August 1807. [SM.69.958]

FAIRBAIRN, PETER, a farmer in Moy, a letter 1826. [NRS.GD46.1.329]

FALCONER, ALEXANDER, from Inverness, graduated MA from King's College, Aberdeen, in March 1838, later a school master at the Cape of Good Hope, South Africa. [KCA]

FALCONER, JAMES, son of William Falconer in Inverness, a student at Marischal College, Aberdeen, in 1820s. [MCA]

FALCONER, JAMES, son of William Falconer in Inverness, a student at Marischal College, Aberdeen, in 1820s. [MCA]

FALCONER, JAMES C., from Inverness, graduated MA from King's College, Aberdeen, in March 1847, a teacher in Jamaica. [KCA]

FALCONER, JOHN, born 1773 in Inverness, late of Drakies, Inverness-shire, the British Consul in Leghorn, [Livorno], Italy, for 30 years, died there on 29 September 1843. [AJ.5006]

FALCONER, WILLIAM, a letter from Kingston, Jamaica, describing his voyage there in 1832, and another from Lentran, Kirkhill in 1840. [NRS.GD23.6.663]

FERGUSON, ALEXANDER, born 1765, died 29 December 1817, husband of Eleanor Grant, born 1772, died 14 October 1818, both were natives of Glen Moriston. [Nine Mile River gravestone, Hants County, Nova Scotia]

FERGUSON, CHARLES, born 1765, a farmer in King Street, Inverness, died 26 August 1849, husband of Jane Cameron, born 1771, died 17 December 1841. [Chapel Yard gravestone, Inverness]

FERGUSON, DAVID, born 1769 in Inverness-shire, died 27 April 1854, husband of Isabella McLeod, born 1785, died 1872. [Millbrook gravestone, Pictou, NS]

FERGUSON, JOHN, born 1798 in Illery, emigrated to America. 1803, settled at Union Church, Moore County, North Carolina, died on 18 December 1858. [N.C. Presbyterian.1.1.1859]

FERGUSON, JOHN, born 1808, shepherd to Alexander Grant the tacksman of Dundreggan, Urquhart, was accused of culpable homicide in 1829. [NRS.AD14.29.348]

FERGUSON, JOHN, born 1857, with wife Agnes born 1866, and son James born 1885, from Inverness, emigrated via Glasgow aboard the Earl Granville bound for Australia on 16 March 1887, landed at Bundaberg, Australia, on 13 July 1887.

FERGUSON, N., born 1790 in Inverness-shire, emigrated to America. 1803, died in Moore County, North Carolina, on 18 December 1864. [N.C. Presbyterian.11.5.1864]

FERGUSON, THOMAS, in Duldreggan, Glen Moriston, was accused of forging and uttering a false bill in 1838. [NRS.AD14.38.24]

FINDLAY, THOMAS, born 1822, died in Clachnacarry on 8 November 1893, husband of Elizabeth MacDonald, born 1825, died 8 March 1866. [Old High gravestone, Inverness]

FINLAYSON, MURDOCH, born 1813, wife Catherine born 1816, and son Malcolm born 1835, from Balmeanach, Raasay, emigrated via Liverpool aboard the Priscilla bound for Victoria, Australia, on 15 October 1852. [NRS.HD4/5]

FLEMING, W., house carpenter, 1837. [Chapel Yard gravestone, Inverness]

FLETCHER, THOMAS, born 1791, a grocer in Young Street, Inverness, was accused of forging and uttering a false bill in 1838. [NRS.AD14.38.24]

FLORENCE, JAMES, born 1803, an accountant in the Bank of Scotland in Inverness, died 26 May 1836. [Chapel Yard gravestone, Inverness]

FLYTER, DUNCAN, a Lieutenant of the 41st Regiment of Native Infantry, second son of Robert Flyter the Sheriff substitute at Fort William, died at Chicacole in the Madras Presidency on 31 March 1831. [S.15.1236]

FLYTER, ROBERT, a writer in Edinburgh, son of Robert Flyter a weaver in Dykeside, was admitted as a Notary Public on 11 March 1796, later a writer in Fort William and sheriff substitute there, died 12 November 1837. [NRS.NP2.35.315]

FLYTER, ROBERT, factor of Badenoch, papers 1822. [NRS.GD44.51.23.3]

FORBES, ALEXANDER, born 1780 in Inverness-shire, died in Merigomish, Nova Scotia, on 1 September 1842. [Halifax Morning Post, 13.9.1842]

FORBES, ALEXANDER, son of Duncan Forbes, [1783-1839], a blacksmith, and his wife Isabella Johnston, [1792-1874] a merchant in San Francisco, California. [Old High Church gravestone, Inverness]; testament, 1884. [NRS.SC70.1.230/603]

FORBES, ARTHUR, of Culloden, born 25 January 1819, died 16 March 1879, husband of Louisa Sarah Georgina, born 3 July 1830, died 19 December 1896. [Chapel Yard gravestone, Inverness]

FORBES, DAVID, a thief who was sentenced at Inverness to seven years transportation to the colonies in 1816. [NRS.GD1.959]

FORBES, DONALD, was granted a tack of Midtown of Duntelchaig, for nineteen years in 1839. [NRS.GD176.1453]

FORBES, DONALD, born 3 April 1766, tenant farmer of Wester Erchite later of Mid Duntelchaig, died 24 April 1843, husband of Mary Fraser, parents of James Forbes, born 26 February 1817, died in Berbice on 31 October 1838. [Dores gravestone]

FORBES, DONALD, born 1773, farmer at Burnside of Holm, died 7 January 1859, husband of Catherine Fraser, born 1779, died 11 January 1848, parents of Donald Forbes, born 1810, died in Ireland in September 1850. [Dores gravestone]

FORBES, DUNCAN, of Culloden, born 7 May 1821, died 8 April 1897. [Chapel Yard gravestone, Inverness]

FORBES, JAMES, born 1799, son of James Forbes a merchant in Inverness, resident of Demerara for 16 years, died there on 29 December 1830. [AJ.4338]

FORBES, JAMES, son of Alexander Forbes a labourer in Lymuick, Alvie, a horse and cattle thief in 1843. [NRS.AD14.43.23]

FORBES, JOHN, and his wife Winwood Mackintosh, in Wester Raitts, testament, 20 May 1794, Comm. Inverness. [NRS]

FORBES, WILLIAM, from Strathglass, emigrated to Nova Scotia in 1801. [NLS.ms96446/41]

FORBES, WILLIAM, born 1758, in Kilmoraig, emigrated to Nova Scotia in 1801, died 4 March 1838. [Caledonia gravestone, Pictou, NS]

FOWLER, ALPIN GRANT, eldest son of Reverend James Fowler in Urquhart, married Ann Margaret Thomson, only daughter of Dr

Robert Thomson in Demerara, in Georgetown, Demerara, on 13 June 1838. [AJ.4727]

FOWLER, CHARLES, born 1782 in the Black Isle, was apprenticed to Charles Jamieson, a goldsmith in Inverness, in 1798. [Inverness Hammermen's Minute Book]

FRANCE, PETER, son of George France a farmer in Kirkhill, a student at Marischal College, Aberdeen, in 1843. [MCA]

FRASER, ALEXANDER, born 1755 in Kilmorack, emigrated to Nova Scotia in 1775, died 8 September 1828, husband of Mary McDonald born 1773, died 1849. [Pioneer gravestone, Pictou, NS]

FRASER, ALEXANDER, born 1770, died in Easter Glackton on 22 December 1849, husband of Margaret Fraser, born 1772, died 8 April 1854. [Brachlich gravestone]

FRASER, ALEXANDER, born 1801 in Kiltarlity, emigrated to Nova Scotia in 1801, died 11 January 1846, husband of Mary Gordon, born 1801 in Inverness-shire, died 6 January 1872. [Hill gravestone, Pictou, NS]

FRASER, ALEXANDER, tacksman of Kiltarlity, with Medley, Mary [born 1789], Elizabeth [born 1795], and Margaret [born 1798], emigrated via Fort William aboard the Sarah of Liverpool bound for Pictou, Nova Scotia, in June 1801. [NRS.RH2.4.87]

FRASER, ALEXANDER, born 1784, a mason in Inverness, died 29 November 1846, husband of Mary Chisholm, born 1784, died 8 February 1844. [Kirkton of Bunchrew gravestone]

FRASER, ALEXANDER, and his wife, from Fort Augustus, emigrated via Fort William aboard the Friends of Saltcoats master John How to Montreal in July 1802. [GkAd.59]

FRASER, ALEXANDER R., born 1797 in Inverness-shire, emigrated to Nova Scotia in 1818, died 1832, husband of Annabella Munro, born 1799, died 1829. [Caledonia gravestone, Pictou, NS]

FRASER, ALEXANDER, from Inverness, graduated MA from King's College, Aberdeen, in March 1826. [KCA]

FRASER, ALEXANDER J., from Inverness, graduated MA from King's College, Aberdeen, in March 1838. [KCA]

FRASER, ALEXANDER, tenant in Campbellton, Ardesier, letters re illegal fishing in 1831. [NRS.GD23.6.666]

FRASER, ALEXANDER, son of Simon Fraser in Fort George died on 31 January 1841. [Kirkton of Ardersier gravestone]

FRASER, ALEXANDER, blacksmith in Culduthel, died 1842, husband of Janet Fraser, grandparents of Alexander Maclean in Waiho, Waimate, New Zealand. [Old High gravestone, Inverness]

FRASER, ALISTER, from Affleck of Culduthel, a student at Marischal College, Aberdeen, in 1845. [MCA]

FRASER, ANDREW, born 1775 in Inverness, a crofter and a pauper in Dunain in 1857, father of several children including John Fraser born 1823 a labourer who emigrated to Canada. [IPR]

FRASER, Major ANDREW, of Flemington, born 6 April 1779 at Ardgay, Fort Major and Governor of Fort George for 35 years, died there on 20 December 1846, husband of Annabella Campbell, born 9 November 1798 at Fort George, died in Inverness on 19 October 1862, parents of Leopold Saxe Cobourg Fraser, born at Fort George on 3 September 1819, a Lieutenant of the Ceylon Rifle Brigade, who died in Columbo, Ceylon, on 1 December1846. [Kirkton of Ardersier gravestone]

FRASER, ANDREW, a merchant in Inverness, 1801.
[NRS.B59.38.6.200.5]

FRASER, ANDREW, son of John Fraser, [1749-1802], a weaver, and
his wife Isabella Grant, [1741-1799], died in the West Indies.
[Chapel Yard gravestone, Inverness]

FRASER, ANGUS, in Balnaglack of Petty, testament, 27 November
1800, Comm. Inverness. [NRS]

FRASER, ANGUS, in Demerara, son of Alexander Fraser of
Ballindern, an inventory, 1839. [NRS.GD23.10.732]

FRASER, ANN, with Margaret Fraser, from Ereless, emigrated via Fort
William aboard the Sarah of Liverpool bound for Pictou, Nova Scotia, in
June 1801. [NRS.RH2.4.87]

FRASER, Mrs ANN, born 1800 in Inverness, wife of Alexander Fraser,
died in Halifax, New Brunswick, on 4 August 1838. [Halifax Pearl,
10.8.1838]

FRASER, or GRANT, ANN, born 1777 in Glen Urquhart, a servant
now a pauper in Shoe Lane, Merkinch, in 1857, mother of several
children including John born 1827 now in Australia. [IPR]

FRASER, ARCHIBALD, son of Frederick Fraser a gentleman of the
Lovat family, a student at Marischal College around 1815, later of
Abertarff. [MCA]

FRASER, CATHERINE, from Strathglass, emigrated via Fort William
aboard the Sarah of Liverpool bound for Pictou, Nova Scotia, in June
1801. [NRS.RH2.4.87]

FRASER, CATHERINE, eldest daughter of Reverend Alexander Fraser
in Inverness, married Hugh Denoon, in Pictou, Nova Scotia, in 1819.
[BM.5.373]; relict of Hugh Denoon of Belleville, the Collector of
Customs, died in Pictou, N.S. on 11 November 1838. [SG.8.735]

FRASER, CATHERINE, born 1803, daughter of James B. Fraser of Gorthleck, Stratherrick, and wife of Alexander Fraser jr., died at Miramichi, New Brunswick, on 20 January 1842. [NBC.29.1.1842]

FRASER, CHARLES, from Inverness, graduated MA from King's College, Aberdeen, in March 1831. [KCA]

FRASER, COLIN, [1829-1903], a farmer, husband of Catherine Fraser, [1842-1918], parents of John Fraser, born 1867, died in Port Huron, USA, on 9 March 1915. [Drumnadrochit gravestone]

FRASER, DANIEL, a commission agent and merchant in New York, second son of Robert Fraser of Kilcoy in Berbice, formerly a merchant in Inverness, died in Thompsonville, Connecticut, on 22 August 1869. [S.8150]

FRASER, DAVID, MA, minister at Dores from 1823 to 1844. [F.6.451]

FRASER, DAVID, born 1817, farmer in Balblair, died 7 January 1896, husband of Ann Mckintosh, born 1822, died 7 September 1905. [Bracklich gravestone]

FRASER, DONALD, born 1723, a gardener in Inverness, died 10 December 1803, husband of Isobel Elder, born 1728, died 17 January 1804, parents of William Fraser a shoemaker in Inverness. [Chapel Yard gravestone, Inverness]

FRASER, DONALD, a smith in Achnafouran, Arisaig, with family, emigrated via Arisaig aboard the British Queen bound for Quebec on 16 August 1790. [PAC.RG4A1, Vol.48.PP15874-5]

FRASER, DONALD, son of Alexander Fraser minister of Kirkhill, graduated MA from Marischal College, Aberdeen, in 1800, later minister at Kirkhill. [MCA]

FRASER, DONALD, born 1781 in Inverness-shire, died in 1827. [Midway gravestone, Georgia]

FRASER, DONALD, a writer in Inverness, testament, August 1799, Comm. Inverness. [NRS]

FRASER, DONALD, on the Muir of Inglishtown, died 3 May 1813, husband of Kathrin Fraser who died on 24 December 1816. [Kirkton of Nunchrew gravestone]

FRASER, DONALD, with his wife and one child, from Leck, emigrated via Fort William aboard the Friends of Saltcoats, master John How, to Montreal in July 1802. [GkAd.59]

FRASER, DONALD, born 1781 in Inverness-shire, emigrated to Nova Scotia in 1820, died 26 February 1868. [Hill gravestone, Pictou, NS]

FRASER, DONALD, born 1782 in Inverness-shire, emigrated to Nova Scotia in 1803, settled at West River, died 21 January 1859. [Oak Grove gravestone, Pictou, NS]

FRASER, DONALD, from Inverness, graduated MA from King's College, Aberdeen, in March 1838, later minister of the Free Church in Cromdale. [KCA]

FRASER, DONALD, the younger, from Inverness, graduated MA from King's College, Aberdeen, in March 1842, later minister of the Free Church in Montreal, Inverness, and London. [KCA]

FRASER, DONALD, was granted a tack of Milton of Tordarroch, for fourteen years in 1846. [NRS.GD176.1453]

FRASER, DONALD, born 1785, a wright at Clachnaharry by the Caledonian Canal, died 12 February 1853, husband of Mary Ann Umpherston. [Wardlaw gravestone]

FRASER, DONALD, jr., an ironmonger in Inverness, accounts, 1849-1853. [NRS.GD176.1688]

FRASER, DUNCAN, born in Inverness around 1780, a soldier, settled in Megantic County, Quebec, in 1824. [AMC.35]

FRASER, DUNCAN, born 1736, a gardener in Auchnagairn, died 12 April 1825, husband of Margaret Wishart, born 1740, died 15 December 1807, parents of Donald Fraser a nurseryman in Inverness, and John Fraser who died at Morton Bay, New South Wales, Australia, aged 32. [Wardaw gravestone]

FRASER, DUNCAN, born 1804, died 3 May 1888, husband of Ann Fraser, born 1815, died 1 October 1871, parents of Mary Fraser, born 1857, died in New Zealand in 1875. [Dores gravestone]

FRASER, EWAN, and his son Alexander Fraser, were granted a tack of Polcher, Strathnairn, for nineteen years in 1839. [NRS.GD176.1453]

FRASER, FANNY, born 1841, wife of Lewis Thering, died in San Francisco, California, on 19 December 1860. [Old High Church gravestone, Inverness]

FRASER, FRANCES, born 12 December 1781 in Inverness, daughter of James and Mary Fraser, married Samuel Corrie, settled in Charleston, South Carolina, in 1784, died 13 March 1850. [Old Scots gravestone, Charleston]

FRASER, FANNY, born 1841, daughter of Lockhart Fraser, wife of Lewis Thering, died in California on 19 December 1860. [Old High gravestone, Inverness]

FRASER, HUGH, born in Kiltarlity, emigrated to Pictou, Nova Scotia, on the Hector in 1773, settled by the East River in May 1774, died on 25 July 1826. [Iron Bridge gravestone, New Glasgow, N.S.]

FRASER, HUGH, in Crunaglack of Strathglass, testament, 20 October 1797, Comm. Inverness. [NRS]

FRASER, HUGH, from Inverness, graduated MA from King's College, Aberdeen, on 30 March 1801, later a minister. [KCA]

FRASER, HUGH, a wright in Glashan, Kiltarlity, was accused of theft in 1812. [NRS.AD14.12.35]

FRASER, HUGH, from Inverness, graduated MA from King's College, Aberdeen, on28 March 1812, later schoolmaster at Kirkhill. [KCA]

FRASER, HUGH, versus Reverend Donald Fraser and the heritors of Kirkhill in 1829. [NRS.CS271.54476]

FRASER, HUGH, in Muirton, died 24 April 1831, husband of Janet Fraser, parents of William in Canada. [Kirkton of Bunchrew gravestone]

FRASER, HUGH, born 1788 in Inverness-shire, settled at Mount Thom, Nova Scotia, died 7 December 1860, husband of Mary Stuart, born 1792, died 1861. [Caledonia gravestone, Pictou, NS]

FRASER, General Sir HUGH, versus George Sutar the tacksman of Redcastle Mains, Beauly, 1838. [NRS.CS46.1838.5.29]

FRASER, HUGH, from Inverness, graduated MA from King's College, Aberdeen, in March 1839. [KCA]

FRASER, HUGH, was accused of profanity at Kirkhill parish church in 1839, trial papers. [NRS.JC26.1939.126]

FRASER, ISABELLA, daughter of Colonel James Fraser of Belladrum, and Thomas Cuming in Demerara, a marriage contract dated 1798. [NRS.RD5.31.279]; they were married at Culladrum on 6 September 1798. [EA.3622.175]

FRASER, ISABELL, in Inverness, 1850, widow of Thomas Frederick Rankin, MD, a sasine. [NRS.RS38.PR54.268]

FRASER, ISABELLA, born 1806 in Inverness-shire, died on 5 November 1881, wife of Kenneth Davidson, born 1774, died 1874. [Hill gravestone, Pictou County, NS]

FRASER, JAMES, from Culmin, Kiltarlity, paymaster of the Royal Artillery in New York, a sasine, 1782. [NRS.RS.Inverness.34]

FRASER, JAMES, in Ballintore, testament, 14 April 1794, Comm. Inverness. [NRS]

FRASER, JAMES, son of James Fraser of Belladrum, a planter in Demerara in 1795. [NRS.GD23.5.352]

FRASER, JAMES, born 1757, emigrated in 1804, settled in Drummond, Pictou, Nova Scotia, died in 1838. [Inverness Courier, 13.2.1839]

FRASER, JAMES, from Inverness, graduated MA from King's College, Aberdeen, on 10 March 1801. [KCA]

FRASER, JAMES BAILLIE, of Ballindoun and Kinnares, account, 1813. [NRS.GD23.10.685]

FRASER, JAMES, born 1761 in Inverness, a merchant in Halifax, Nova Scotia, died 14 October 1822, probate 1822, Halifax, N.S.; father of James de Wolf Fraser, a sasine 1824. [NRS.RS.Inverness.231/249]

FRASER, JAMES, from Craggach, Kirkhill, later in Urbana, Middlesex, Virginia, testament, 1836. [NRS.GD23.10.727]

FRASER, JAMES, born 1749 in Inverness, settled in Charleston, South Carolina, in 1785, died there on 24 April 1842. [Old Scots gravestone, Charleston.]

FRASER, JAMES, born 1754 in Inverness, emigrated in 1804, died in Drummond on the West Branch of the East River, Pictou, Nova Scotia, on 12 April 1838. [Acadian Recorder, 28.4.1838] [IJ.13.2.1839]

FRASER, JAMES, born 1791, died in Hill Terrace, Inverness, on 30 January 1881, husband of Margaret Fraser, born 1790, died on 24 October 1851. [Chapel Yard gravestone, Inverness]

FRASER, JAMES, born 1808 in Skye, a deserter from the 93rd Regiment of Foot, accused of housebreaking in Dunning, Perthshire, in 1836. [NRS.AD14]

FRASER, JAMES, a labourer in Inverness, died in February 1849, father of James Fraser a painter in New York. [NRS.S/H]

FRASER, JAMES, born 1837, son of Lockhart Fraser, died 11 April 1862. [Old High gravestone, Inverness]

FRASER, JAMES, born 1760, in Dromchardinie, died 4 June 1833, husband of Catherine ......, parents of Alexander Fraser in Ceylon, and Thomas Fraser in Drumchardinie. [Wardlaw gravestone]

FRASER, JAMES, died 1846, and his wife Catherine, died 1846, in Baddan, Kiltarlity, parents of Andrew Fraser who settled in Embo, Canada, before 1887, also of John Fraser who died in Embo in 1870. [Glen Convinth gravestone]

FRASER, JAMES, a painter in New York, son and heir of James Fraser a labourer in Inverness, who died in February 1849. [NRS.S/H]

FRASER, JANE, born 1831 in Stromness, married William Spence in Stromness on 27 February 1851, died in Victoria, British Columbia, on 13 September 1875. [Ross Bay gravestone]

FRASER, JANE, born 1832, wife of William Grant, died in Templestove, Ceylon, on 6 March 1863. [Rothiemurchus gravestone]

FRASER, JANE, fifth daughter of William Fraser in Clunas, widow of A. Stewart, married Thomas Hogan from Buckhorn, Louisiana, at Milliken's Bend, La., on 13 September 1877. [EC.29031]

FRASER, JANET, from Inverness-shire, married James Doyle in Halifax, Nova Scotia, on 10 February 1835. [AR.14.2.1835]

FRASER, JANET, born 1777 in Inverness, a widow and a pauper in Clachnaharry, mother of several children including Simon born 1817 who settled in Australia. [IPR]

FRASER, JEMIMA JOHNSTONE, daughter of John Fraser of Farraline, died in Toronto, Canada, on 18 September 1848. [SG.1760]

FRASER, or DUFF, JESS, born 1801, a widow and a pauper in Wright's Lane, Inverness, in 1857, mother of several children including Eliza born 1825 who settled in America. [IPR]

FRASER. JOHN, born 1761, died in Halifax, Nova Scotia, on 14 October 1822, probate 19 October 1822, Halifax, N.S.

FRASER, JOHN OGG, tenant in Ballindalloch of Farraline, and his wife Janet Fraser, [1745-1812], parents of John Fraser a merchant in Halifax, Nova Scotia. [Old Boleskine gravestone]

FRASER, JOHN, of Garthmore, testament, 3 July 1790, Comm. Inverness. [NRS]

FRASER, JOHN, born 1765 in Kiltarlity, died 23 February 1842. [Hill gravestone, Pictou, NS]

FRASER, JOHN, a merchant in New York, a sasine 1782. [NRS.RS.Inverness.34]

FRASER, JOHN HUTCHISON, a barrister in Jamaica, son and heir of Captain Simon Fraser of Fanellan in 1793. [NRS.S/H]

FRASER, JOHN, from Inverness, graduated MA from King's College, Aberdeen, on 28 March 1799. [KCA]

FRASER, JOHN, a labourer from Kirkhill, with Christian, and Isobel born 1799, emigrated via Fort William aboard the Sarah of Liverpool bound for Pictou, Nova Scotia, in June 1801. [NRS.RH2.4.87]

FRASER, JOHN, born 1769 in Inverness, a merchant in South Carolina, was naturalised on 16 March 1807. [NARA.M1183.1]

FRASER, JOHN, born 1785 in Inverness, a merchant, was naturalised in South Carolina on 26 February 1810. [NARA.M1183.1]

FRASER, JOHN, [1749-1802], a weaver, husband of Isabella Grant, [1741-1799], parents of Andrew Fraser and William Fraser who both died in the West Indies. [Chapel Yard gravestone, Inverness]

FRASER, JOHN, a farmer from Kiltarlity, with Christian, William a labourer, Bell, Ann [born 1798], emigrated via Fort William aboard the Sarah of Liverpool bound for Pictou, Nova Scotia, in June 1801. [NRS.RH2.4.87]

FRASER, JOHN, born 1776, a wine merchant in Inverness, died on 18 December 1803. [Chapel Yard gravestone, Inverness]

FRASER, JOHN, agent for the Bank of Scotland in Inverness, a sasine of the lands of Dalcromby and Letterdrillan, Strathnain, in 1807. [NRS.CS228.F8.29]

FRASER, JOHN, a wright in Dalnamine, was accused of theft in 1812. [NRS.AD14.12.35]

FRASER, JOHN, born 1764, a Preacher of the Gospel, died 27 July 1792, husband of Mary Ogilvie, born 1761, died 12 January 1803. [Chapel Yard gravestone, Inverness]

FRASER, JOHN, from Inverness, graduated MA from King's College, Aberdeen, on 28 March 1812, later schoolmaster at Tomintoul. [KCA]

FRASER, JOHN, born 1810, farmer at Wester Erchite, Dores, died 1 August 1892, husband of Elizabeth Fraser, born 1829, died 25 April 1912, parents of John Fraser, born 1855, died at Mabel Bush, New Zealand, on 9 August 1927. [Dores gravestone]

FRASER, JOHN, a merchant from Inverness, married Margaret McArthur, fifth daughter of John McArthur of Sussex Vale, New Brunswick, in Chatham, N.B., on 8 August 1843. [New Brunswick Courier, 19.8.1843]

FRASER, or MCIVER, JOHN, in Achblair, Kilmorack, was found guilty of assaulted and was outlawed in 1836. [NRS.JC11.84]

FRASER, JOHN, born 1837 in Inverness, died in New York on 15 April 1856. [CM.20784]

FRASER, JOHN, former Provost of Inverness, later an agent of the Montreal Bank in Chatham, Western District, Canada, in 1844. [IC.4.9.1844]

FRASER, JOHN, a merchant in Inverness, became a Commissioner in Canada for the British America Land Company, later a bank agent in London, Canada, a sasine, 1846. [NRS.RS38.PR51.109]

FRASER, JOHN, born 1836, son of Thomas Fraser in Clachnaharry, died in Georgetown, Demerara, on 10 November 1866. [Old High gravestone, Inverness]

FRASER, LOCKHART, born 1800, a house carpenter, died 10 July 1889, husband of Hannah Fraser, born 1803, died 20 October 1885. [Old High gravestone, Inverness]

FRASER, MARGARET, born in Inverness-shire around 1778, wife of Donald McDonald, emigrated to Nova Scotia in 1832. [New Glasgow gravestone, N.S.]

FRASER, MARGARET, daughter of John Fraser of Farraline an advocate, died in Hamilton, Upper Canada, on 23 September 1847. [AJ.5207]

FRASER, MARY, daughter of Captain Robertson in Inverness, married Roderick Matheson, late of the Glengarry Light Infantry, in Montreal, Quebec, on 5 November 1823. [FH.132]

FRASER, Mrs MARY, born 1746 in Inverness, wife of James Fraser, died in South Carolina on 25 November 1836. [Old Scots gravestone, Charleston]

FRASER, REBECCA HARIOT, daughter of John Fraser of Farraline an advocate in Inverness, married Reverend John Gray in Toronto, Canada, on 27 August 1850. [AJ.5362]; she died in Kingston, Canada West, on 10 February 1851. [W.1200] [FJ.950] [GM.NS35.455]

FRASER, ROBERT, from Inverness, graduated MA from King's College, Aberdeen, on 10 March 1801. [KCA]

FRASER, SIMON, youngest son of William Fraser of Culbuckie, formerly a Captain in the Glengarry Fencibles, died in Bermuda where he had gone to from St Vincent, on 12 October 1798. [EA.3675.183]

FRASER, SIMON, born 1789, a merchant in Inverness, died 25 March 1867, husband of Margaret Strother, born 1809, died 1 August 1865. [Chapel Yard gravestone, Inverness]

FRASER, SIMON, from Inverness, graduated MA from King's College, Aberdeen, on 10 March 1801. [KCA]

FRASER, SIMON, eldest son of Donald Fraser of Balloan, settled on the Golden Fleece Plantation in Berbice, died there on 15 September 1803. [DPCA.72]

FRASER, Captain SIMON, of Fanellan, dead by 1793, father of John Hutchison Fraser a barrister in Jamaica. [NRS.S/H]

FRASER, SIMON, minister at Glenmoriston from 1799 until 1815. [F.6.453]

FRASER, SIMON, from Inverness-shire, emigrated to Nova Scotia in 1803. [New Glasgow gravestone, N.S.]

FRASER, SIMON, from Inverness, graduated MA from King's College, Aberdeen, on 31 March 1806. [KCA]

FRASER, SIMON, jr., a merchant in Quebec, son of Hugh Fraser of Dell, Inverness-shire, a sasine, 1789. [NRS.RS.Inverness.275]

FRASER, SIMON, born 1789, tacksman of Canteen, Fort George, died 7 March 1849, husband of Isabella Forbes at Fort George, died 9 May 1834. [Kirkton of Ardersier gravestone]

FRASER, SIMON, a labourer from Kilmorack, with Ann, emigrated via Fort William aboard the Sarah of Liverpool bound for Pictou, Nova Scotia, in June 1801. [NRS.RH2.4.87]

FRASER, SIMON, the younger, from Inverness, graduated MA from King's College, Aberdeen, in April 1829, later minister of the Free Church in Fortrose. [KCA]

FRASER, SIMON, born 1834, son of William Fraser, a farmer Clunes, and his wife Helen Fraser, died in Somerset, South Africa, on 11 December 1861. [Wardlaw gravestone]

FRASER, SIMON, born 1853, son of John Fraser and his wife Jessie Tolmie, died in Denver, Colorado, on 11 December 1888. [Tomnacross, Kiltarlity, gravestone]

FRASER, SUSAN, eldest daughter of Simon Fraser of Kilmorack, [Cill Mhoraig], married W. Katz, in Berbice on 9 January 1826. [EA]

FRASER, THOMAS, born 1765 in Kirkhill, graduated MA from King's College, Aberdeen, in 1788, a teacher at Inverness Academy, ordained in 1796, a minister in Inverness from 1801 until his death on 3 February 1834. [F.6.458]

FRASER, THOMAS, Captain of the 14th Regiment, died in Norfolk, Virginia, son of Simon Fraser of Fannallan, admin. 1790, PCC. [TNA]

FRASER, THOMAS, the tacksman of Knockchoilum, testament, 3 July 1790, Comm. Inverness. [NRS]

FRASER, THOMAS, in Chateau Belair, St David's, St Vincent, from Kiltarlity, Inverness-shire, appointed Simon Fraser of Bobleving as his factor in 1797. [NRS.RD4.261.1247]

FRASER, THOMAS, born 1808, a shoemaker in Inverness, died 28 January 1855, husband of Mary Cameron. [Od High gravestone, Inverness]

FRASER, THOMAS, in Clachnaharry, born 1795, died 11 March 1895, husband of Anne Wishart, born 1802, died 2 May 1854. [Old High gravestone, Inverness]

FRASER, THOMAS, born 1824, third son of Thomas Fraser and his wife Jane Sutar, died in Mandeville, Jamaica, on 1 June 1860. [Inverness, Chapel Yard gravestone][S.1571]

FRASER, THOMAS, from Inverness, graduated MA from King's College, Aberdeen, in March 1835. [KCA]

FRASER, THOMAS MCKENZIE, from Inverness, graduated MA from King's College, Aberdeen, in March 1842, later a Free Church minister in Yester. [KCA]

FRASER, WILLIAM, born 1777, a farmer in Lannwelig, Almy, with his wife Janet, born 1782, and children Thomas, born 1804, and Ann, born 1806, emigrated aboard the George of New York bound for N.Y. on 12 August 1807. [TNA.PC1.3790]

FRASER, WILLIAM, Church of Scotland missionary at Fort William from 1790 to 1793, minister at Boleskine and Abertarff from 1800 until his death 7 June 1840, husband of Robina McBrayne, parents of William Fraser, born 1814 who went to Canada, and others. [F.6.446]

FRASER, WILLIAM, born 1798, in Clunes, died 29 June 1869, husband of Helen Fraser, born 1803, died 17 December 1870, parents of Peter Fraser of the Royal Sappers and Miners, born 1824, died in Stornaway on 11 February 1851, Simon Fraser, born 1834, died in Somerset, South Africa on 11 December 1861, John Fraser, born 1836, died 1838, and other brothers in Byaduk, Australia. [Wardlaw gravestone]

FRASER, WILLIAM, tacksman of Ullarhust of Petty, subscribed to a bond of caution for Hugh Sinclair the miller at the Milton of Ladich of Petty in 1803. [NRS.CS271.571]

FRASER, WILLIAM, born 1759, vintner of the Inverness Mason Lodge, died 11 January 1802, husband of Jean Fraser. [Chapel Yard gravestone, Inverness]

FRASER, Reverend WILLIAM, in Arisaig, a letter, 28 March 1808. [NRS.NRAS.2177, bundle 1532]

FRASER, WILLIAM, born 1801, farmer in Craggie, died 17 April 1889, husband of Marjory Colvin, born 1806, died 2 June 1846. [Dores gravestone]

FRASER, WILLIAM, born 1836, farmer in Craggie, died 17 November 1905, husband of Marjory Clunas, born 1840, died 8 September 1874. [Dores gravestone]

FRASER, WILLIAM, son of John Fraser, [1749-1802], a weaver, and his wife Isabella Grant, [1741-1799], died in the West Indies. [Chapel Yard gravestone, Inverness]

FRASER, WILLIAM, born 13 March 1753 in Inverness, died on 25 April 1826 in Troy, New York. [Old Troy gravestone]

FRASER, WILLIAM, in Torgormack, Kilmorack, and Simon Calder, son of John Calder in Torgormack, were accused of assaulting Revenue Officers in 1820. [NRS.JC26.1820.4]

FRASER, WILLIAM, from Inverness, graduated MA from King's College, Aberdeen, in March 1837. [KCA]

FRASER, WILLIAM, from Inverness, graduated MA from King's College, Aberdeen, in March 1843, later a schoolmaster in Auchterhouse. [KCA]

FRASER, WILLIAM, youngest son of Reverend Thomas Fraser in Inverness, died in Henrietta, Demerara, on 13 September 1845. [AJ.5108]

FRASER, WILLIAM, son of Hugh Fraser, a farmer in Muirton, [died 24 April 1831], and his wife Janet Fraser, settled in Canada. [Kirkton of Bunchew gravestone]

FRASER, WILLIAM, born 1813, son of Reverend Simon Fraser in Kilmorack, died in Beaufort West, Cape of Good Hope, South Africa, in October 1863. [AJ.6058]

FRASER, W., late in Quebec, died in Inverness on 15 September 1873. [Chapel Yard gravestone, Inverness]

FYVIE, CHARLES, born 1795, Dean of Moray and Ross, Episcopal pastor in Inverness for 30 years, died 13 February 1849, husband of Janet Adam, born 1796, died 14 July 1828. [Chapel Yard gravestone, Inverness]

GARDEN, ALEXANDER, born 1808, died 18 August 1849, husband of Elizabeth Melven. [Old High gravestone, Inverness]

GARDEN, JOHN, in Dalnavert, Alvie, accused of falsehood in 1819. [NRS.AD14.19.14]

GARDNER, WILLIAM BETHELL, Major General, Royal Artillery, born 19 August 1815, died 15 June 1880, husband of Eliza Augusta...., born 22 January 1820, died 19 September 1878. [Brachlich gravestone]

GELLION, ARTHUR GEORGE, born 1819, son of Thomas Gellion. [1781-1840], and his wife Helen McKinnon, [1782-1829], died in Dominica, British West Indies, on 25 April 1858. [Chapel Yard gravestone, Inverness]

GELLION, JOHN, born 1811, son of Thomas Gellion in Inverness [1781-1840] and his wife Helen McKinnon, [1782-1829], died in Melbourne, Australia, on7 March 1884. [Chapel Yard gravestone, Inverness]

GELLION, THOMAS, born 1820, son of Thomas Gellion. [1781-1840], and his wife Helen McKinnon, [1782-1829], died in Berbice on 26 August 1837. [Chapel Yard gravestone, Inverness]

GILCHRIST, EBENEZER, manager of the British Linen Company, versus Barbara Robertson on Castlehill, Inverness, and Chritine Robertson in Nairn, 1821. [NRS.CS44.1.12]

GILLAN, JAMES, from Inverness, a planter in St John's parish, Antigua, dead by 1797. [ANY.I.148]

GILLESPIE, THOMAS, in Ardochy, Fort Augustus, testamentary papers, 1823. [NRS.GD23.7.50]

GILLIS, ALEXANDER, a labourer from Arisaig, emigrated via Fort William on board the Dove of Aberdeen bound for Pictou, Nova Scotia, in 1801. [NRS.RH2.4.87.75-5]

GILLIES, ANGUS, a labourer in Morar, Mary Gillies a spinner, emigrated via Fort William on board the Dove of Aberdeen bound for Pictou, Nova Scotia, in 1801. [NRS.RH2.4.87.75-5]

GILLIS, DONALD, born 1760 in Inverness, husband of Catherine McLeod, emigrated to America in 1803, a tailor and farmer in North Carolina. [NCSA.2.75]

GILLIES, DUNCAN, tenant of Ronasick, North Morar, with family, emigrated via Arisaig aboard the British Queen bound for Quebec on 16 August 1790. [PAC.RG4A1, VOL.48.PP15874]

GILLIS, DUNCAN, his wife and four children, emigrated via Fort William aboard the Friends of Saltcoats master John How to Montreal in July 1802. [GkAd.59]

GILLIES, EWEN, born 1825, wife Margaret born 1824, daughter Mary born 1851, from St Kilda, emigrated via Liverpool aboard the Priscilla bound for Victoria, Australia, on 15 October 1852. [NRS.HD4/5]

GILLIS, JOHN, tenant of Beorard, North Morar, and family, emigrated via Arisaig aboard the British Queen bound for Quebec on 16 August 1790. [PAC.RG4A1, VOL.48.PP15874-5]

GILLIS, KATHERINE, a spinner from Arisaig, emigrated via Fort William on board the Dove of Aberdeen bound for Pictou, Nova Scotia, in 1801. [NRS.RH2.4.87.75]

GILLIS, MARY, from Leck, emigrated via Fort William aboard the Friends of Saltcoats master John How to Montreal in July 1802. [GkAd.59]

GILMORE, WILLIAM, master of the Janet of Inverness trading with Easdale in 1820. [NRS.E504.17.8]

GILZEAN, THOMAS, Customs Controller at the Port of Inverness in 1817. [NRS.E504.17.8]

GORDON, ALEXANDER, in Kinvinevaig, testament, 20 April 1798, Comm. Inverness. [NRS]

GORDON, ALEXANDER, born 1805, wife Mary born 1806, daughter Christy born 1836, son Peter born 1839, and daughter Margaret born 1843, from Eyre, Skye or Raasay, emigrated via Liverpool aboard the Allison bound for Melbourne, Australia, on 13 September 1852. [NRS.HD4/5]

GORDON, JAMES, a general agent in Inverness, 1841. [NRS.GD206.5.651]

GORDON, JANE, wife of Reverend Donald Fraser minister of Kirkhill, and Mary Grant, widow of Peter Gordon formerly a farmer in Borlum, mother of the deceased Peter Gordon in Plantation Borlum in Berbice, now wife of John McDonald in Achtemrach, Urquhart, granted power of attorney to Alexander Grant of Plantation Good Intent, Demerara, and Lewis Cameron in Demerara, to deal with the assets of the said Peter Gordon, in 1810. [NRS.GD23.10.667]

GORDON, LEWIS GRANT, son of Reverend Alexander Gordon in Daviot, was apprenticed to James Grant a writer [lawyer] in Inverness in 1809. [NRS. GD23.4.247]

GORDON, PETER, born 1776 in Inverness, died in Musquodoboit, Nova Scotia, on 14 December 1841. [Halifax Journal, 27.12.1841]

GORDON, ROBERT, and Helen McDonald, in Faskmore, Laggan, a marriage certificate, dated 14 November 1831. [NRS.CS238.MC.18.10]

GORDON, THOMAS, Customs Controller of Inverness in 1814. . [NRS.E504.17.8]

GOW, WILLIAM, from Fort William, a Special Magistrate of Honduras, died on 28 October 1838. [SG.8.737]

GRAHAM, JOHN, son of Alexander Graham in Scorbreck farm, Skye, accused of theft in 1801. [NRS.JC11.45]

GRANT, ALEXANDER, born 20 May 1734 in Glen Moriston, son of Patrick Grant and his wife Isobel, to America as a Lieutenant of a Highland regiment in 1754, a merchant and politician who died at Castle Grant, Gross Point, near Detroit, Michigan, on 8 May 1813, buried at Sandwich, Upper Canada. [EA.5197.13][DCB]

GRANT, ALEXANDER, a farmer from Urquhart, with Hannah, Alexander [born 1797], and Isabel [born 1800], emigrated via Fort William aboard the Sarah of Liverpool bound for Pictou, Nova Scotia, in June 1801. [NRS.RH2.4.87]

GRANT, ALEXANDER, born 1734 in Glen Moriston, died 18 April 1810, husband of Margaret Mitchell, born 1743 in Glen Moriston, died 7 June 1812. [Nine Mile River gravestone, Hants County, NS]

GRANT, ALEXANDER, with his wife, John Grant, and four children, from Achnanconeran, [Achadh nan Conbhairean], emigrated via Fort William aboard the Friends of Saltcoats master John How to Montreal in July 1802. [GkAd.59]

GRANT, ALEXANDER, born 1781 in Inverallan, Strathspey, Sergeant of the Inverness Militia, and for 40 years was the Principal Burgh Officer of Inverness, died there on 10 June 1864. [Chapel Yard gravestone, Inverness]

GRANT, ALEXANDER, an accountant in Inverness, 1830-1833. [NRS.176.1575]

GRANT, ANGUS, a farmer from Glenmoriston, with Duncan [born 1790], emigrated via Fort William aboard the Sarah of Liverpool bound for Pictou, Nova Scotia, in June 1801. [NRS.RH2.4.87]

GRANT, ANNE, at Tullochgraban, widow of Donald McPherson of Culinleen, testament, 30 January 1799, Comm. Inverness. [NRS]

GRANT, ANNE, with John Grant and one child from Levishie, [Libhisidh], emigrated via Fort William aboard the Friends of Saltcoats master John How to Montreal in July 1802. [GkAd.59]

GRANT, ANN, was accused of theft at Pressmuckerach, Badenoch, Laggan, found guilty and sentenced to penal servitude for life in 1829. [NRS.JC26.1829.83]

GRANT, BEATRICE, in Duthil Manse, a letter to James Grant in Heathfield, Grantown, in 1802. [NRS.GD248.65.1.38]

GRANT, CHARLES, of Glen Elg, versus Reverend Dr Thomas Ross in 1831. [NRS.CS46.1831.2.24]

GRANT, CHARLES, born 1825, a Lieutenant of the Royal Navy, died in February 1848, son of John Grant an auctioneer. [Chapel Yard gravestone, Inverness]

GRANT, DONALD, and his wife, from Dalcataig, [Dail Cataig], emigrated via Fort William aboard the Friends of Saltcoats master John How, to Montreal in July 1802. [GkAd.59]

GRANT, DONALD, a farmer from Urquhart, with Janet, Alexander [born 1792], Christian [born 1795], Isabel [born 1798], emigrated via Fort William aboard the Sarah of Liverpool bound for Pictou, Nova Scotia, in June 1801. [NRS.RH2.4.87]

GRANT, DONALD FRASER, in Cobourg, Canada, heir to his grand-aunt Ann Munro, widow of Adam Hood a housewright in Inverness, who died 27 June 1843; also, heir to his grand-mother Christian Munro, wife of Donald Grant a cooper in Inverness, who died in July 1838. [NRS.S/H]

GRANT, DONALD, Excise Officer at Aird, Beauly, in 1819. [NRS.GD23.6.556]

GRANT, DUNCAN, factor in Urquhart, a letter to Sir James Grant, writes 'as to lands out of lease at Whitsunday, 2 March 1801. "I am at a loss what to say on this head. A spirit of Emigration to America is creeping in amongst the lower Classes of People in this country. Several families are preparing to emigrate against May first along with a Mr. [Hugh] Denoon a brother of Mr. David Denoon, minister of Killearnan, who came lately from America and who proposes to return in May. I hear he brings several families from the Aird, Strathglass and Glenmoriston also. Unluckily it's not the very poorest he brings with him. The best labourers, acre men and a few of the tenants are those that propose going.' Shortage of meal and influence this is having.' [NRS.GD248.3410.10]

GRANT, Captain DUNCAN, of Delshangie, factor of Urquhart, letters, 1795-1801. [NRS.GD248.3409.8]

GRANT, DUNCAN, from Inverness, graduated MA from King's College, Aberdeen, on 25 March 1808, later a minister in Aberdeen, Alves, and Forres, joined the Free Church. [KCA]

GRANT, DUNCAN, in Wester Achnaveran, Glen Moriston, accused of forgery, outlawed in 1810. [NRS.JC11.51]

GRANT, ELIZABETH, from Drumnadrochit, [Druim na Drochaid], emigrated via Fort William aboard the Friends of Saltcoats master John How to Montreal in July 1802. [GkAd.59]

GRANT, ELSPETH, only daughter of Robert Grant of Riemore, Strathspey, testament, 13 October 1796, Comm. Inverness. [NRS]

GRANT, FRANCIS WILLIAM, from Inverness, graduated MA from King's College, Aberdeen, in March 1817. [KCA]

GRANT, Lieutenant GEORGE, at the Croft of Rothiemurcus, testament, 23 September 1795, Comm. Inverness. [NRS]

GRANT, Colonel HUGH, of Moy, versus Mackenzie and Innes in 1817. [NRS.CS36.18.51]

GRANT, ISABELLA, born 1839, daughter of John Grant an auctioneer in Inverness, wife of Lieutenant Sharp of the Inverness Militia, died 24 December 1861. [Chapel Yard gravestone, Inverness]

GRANT, JAMES, born 1777, a pensioner of the 92nd Regiment, died in October 1834, husband of Margaret McPhail born 1797, died in October 1834. [Brachlich gravestone]

GRANT, JAMES, son of Reverend Grant in Kilmonivaig, died in New York on 9 September 1799. [GM.69.993][EA.3740.280]

GRANT, JAMES, in Inverness, 1813. [NRS.GD23.10.685]

GRANT, JAMES, a factor in Inverness, versus Reverend William Smith in Petty in 1814. [NRS.CS40.15.70]

GRANT, JAMES, from Inverness, graduated MA from King's College, Aberdeen, in March 1822, later minister of Cromdale. [KCA]

GRANT, JAMES MURRAY, in Glenmoriston, letters to James Grant of Bught from 1825 to 1826. [NRS.GD23.6.606]; versus James Forbes of Echt in 1825. [NRS.CS271.64064]

GRANT, JAMES, son of William Grant in Duthil, a student at Marischal College, Aberdeen, in 1839. [MCA]

GRANT, JANE, second daughter of John Peter Grant of Rothiemurchus, MP, married Colonel Gervaise Pennington, HEICS, in Rothiemurchus on 17 December 1825. [SM.97.126]

GRANT, JOHN, a coppersmith in Inverness, husband of Naome Cuthbert, parents of Cuthbert Grant, a merchant in Quebec, a sasine, 1790. [NRS.RS.38.336/PR15.404]

GRANT, JOHN, in Jamaica, died 1791, brother of Lieutenant James Grant of Ballentomb, testament, 1794, Comm. Edinburgh. [NRS]

GRANT, Reverend JOHN, in Urquhart, testament, 1 July 1796, Comm. Inverness. [NRS]

GRANT, JOHN, a farmer from Strathglass, with Catherine, James [born 1791], John [born 1793], Alexander [born 1795], Donald [born 1797], emigrated via Fort William aboard the Sarah of Liverpool bound for Pictou, Nova Scotia, in June 1801. [NRS.RH2.4.87]

GRANT, JOHN, a farmer from Urquhart, with Margaret, Alexander a labourer, Donald a labourer, Margaret, Elizabeth, Patrick [born 1795], Catherine [born 1795], William [born 1797], Robert [born 1799], emigrated via Fort William aboard the Sarah of Liverpool bound for Pictou, Nova Scotia, in June 1801. [NRS.RH2.4.87]

GRANT, JOHN, son of Lewis Grant in Inverness, died at Plantation Nesmis on 19 August 1830. [S.1127]

GRANT, JOHN, born 1785, a mason in Inverness, died on 3 April 1852, husband of Elspet Scott, born 1781, died 13 September 1868. [Old High gravestone, Inverness]

GRANT, JOHN, born 1788 in Inverness, emigrated to America in 1800, settled in Portsmouth, New Hampshire, naturalised there in March 1839. [N.H. Court Records]

GRANT, JOHN PETER, of Rothiemurchus, a letter re the Kincardine Volunteers in 1801. [NRS.GD248.3413.10]; a decreet, 1810. [NRS.CS36.1.13]

GRANT, LEWIS, and Company, stationers in Inverness, versus Samuel Taylor a former student of Fortrose Academy, now abroad, and James Murray a writer in Nairn, a decreet, [NRS.CS38.2.139]

GRANT, MARY, Flory Grant, and Isabella Grant, from Duldreggan, emigrated via Fort William aboard the Friends of Saltcoats master John How to Montreal in July 1802. [GkAd.59]

GRANT, MURDOCH, born 19 May 1785, a builder in Fort Augustus, died 2 December 1867, husband of Mary McKillop, born 1802, died 16 December 1885. [Kilchuimen gravestone]

GRANT, P., of Duthil, a letter to James Grant the younger of Bucht in 1802. [NRS.GD23.6.395]

GRANT, PATRICK, of Rothiemurchus, testament, 20 January 1791, Comm. Inverness. [NRS]

GRANT, PATRICK, of Glenmoriston, testament, 12 November 1795, Comm. Inverness. [NRS]

GRANT, PATRICK, a farmer from Glenmoriston, emigrated via Fort William aboard the Sarah of Liverpool bound for Pictou, Nova Scotia, in June 1801. [NRS.RH2.4.87]

GRANT, PATRICK, MA, minister in Inverness in 1800. [F.6.458]

GRANT, PETER, from Inverness, graduated MA from King's College, Aberdeen, on 28 March 1801. [KCA]

GRANT, PETER, a farmer in Balnabar, and his wife Anne McIntosh, parents of Thomas Grant, born 1850, died in New Zealand o 18 June 1883. [Kilmore, Drumnadrochit, gravestone]

GRANT, WILLIAM, a labourer from Kilmorack, emigrated via Fort William aboard the Sarah of Liverpool bound for Pictou, Nova Scotia, in June 1801. [NRS.RH2.4.87]

GRANT, WILLIAM, from Inverness, graduated MA from KiGRANT, WILLIAM, a labourer from Kilmorack, emigrated via Fort William aboard the Sarah of Liverpool bound for Pictou, Nova Scotia, in June 1801. [NRS.RH2.4.87]

GRANT, WILLIAM, from Inverness, graduated MA from King's College, Aberdeen, on 31 March 1806, later a minister at Kirkmichael and Duthill. [KCA]

GRANT, WILLIAM, born 1827, son of John Grant an auctioneer in Inverness, died at sea in August 1855. [Chapel Yard gravestone, Inverness]

GRANT, WILLIAM MURRAY, of Glen Moriston, a petition in 1820. [NRS.CC2.7.68.1]

GRANT, WILLIAM, born 1791, died at Clachnacarry on 19 September 1866, husband of Margaret Fraser, born 1803, died 6 October 1850. [Chapel Yard gravestone, Inverness]

GRANT, WILLIAM MACDOWALL, married Eleanor Fraser, near Inverness on 5 December 1825. [SM.97.126]

GRANT, WILLIAM PETER, of Rothiemurchus, 1826. [NRS.CS227.25]

GRANT, WILLIAM, in Moniack, Kiltarlity, was murdered in 1831. [NRS.AD14.31.36]

GRANT, WILLIAM, son of Alexander Grant, [1747-1805], and his wife Mary MacIntosh, [1750-1812], in Fort Augustus, settled on Green Island, Jamaica, by 1816. [Clach am Imbhir, Invermoriston]

GRAY, JOHN, was accused of neglect of duty and fraud at the Post Office in Beauly, Kilmorack, in 1834, sentenced to six months in prison. [NRS.JC26.1834.92]

GRAY, THOMAS DAVID, from Inverness, son of Professor David Gray of Marischal College deceased, graduated from there in 1859, a chaplain on the Indian Establishment, later vicar of Babraham, Cambridgeshire. [MCA]

GUNN, JAMES, born 1810, died in Prescott, Canada West, on 16 January 1845. [Wardlaw gravestone, Inverness]

HALLIDAY, ELIZABETH, wife of John Forsyth in Fort William, 1819, sister and heir of David Halliday in Jamaica. [NRS.S/H]

HARDIE, JAMES, son of James Hardie a carpenter in Inverness, a student at Marischal College, Aberdeen, in 1830s. [MCA]

HARFORD, MARY, wife of John Munro a servant in Inverness, was accused of murder in 1812. [NRS.AD14.12.12]

HARKNESS, ROBERT, born 1800, Sergeant Major of the 71st Highland Light Infantry, died 2 February 1834. [Kirkton of Ardersier gravestone]

HARROLD, JOHN, born 1803, died 18 January 1871. [Old High gravestone, Inverness]

HAY, BARBARA, at Milltown of Bellimore, testament, 23 November 1793, Comm. Inverness. [NRS]

HAY, Captain JAMES, born 1841, son of William Hay, [1788-1860], and his wife Isobella Brander, [1799-1872], master of the barque Scottish Chief, was drowned in the Gulf of Florida on 14 April 1881. [Urquhart gravestone]

HAY, JANE, born 1779, daughter of William Hay, farmer in Newtown of Ardesier, and his wife Margaret Shaw, died 24 December 1857. [Brachlich gravestone]

HAYMAN, WILLIAM, from Inverness, emigrated to America before 1776, a soldier of the Royal North Carolina Regiment from 1779 to 1783, moved to Tatamaguche, Nova Scotia, died in 1829. [HT]

HENDERSON, ARCHIBALD, and his wife, from Glen Coe, emigrated via Fort William aboard the Friends of Saltcoats master John How to Montreal in July 1802. [GkAd.59]

HENDRY, CATHERINE, daughter of John Hendry, [1820-1872], a builder in Dores, and his wife Margaret Fraser, [1817-1911], died in Texas on 16 February 1876. [Dores gravestone]

HOOD, JAMES, master of the Lizard of Inverness trading with Leith in 1812. [NRS.E504.17.8]

HUISTON, JAMES, from Inverness, graduated MA from King's College, Aberdeen, on 2 April 1804. [KCA]

HUNTER, WILLIAM, of Glen Moriston, died 1816. [NRS.CS96.1675]

HUTCHESON, PETER, a merchant in Campbellton, Fort George, a decreet, 1815. [NRS.CS36.13.41]

IMLACH, JAMES, a Lieutenant on half pay of the 43rd Light Infantry, barrack master of Fort Augustus, 1820-1821. [NRS.GD51.6.753.1-3]

IMRAY, JOHN, from Inverness, graduated MA from King's College, Aberdeen, in March 1831. [KCA]

INGLIS, HELEN, born 1760, daughter of Hugh Inglis a merchant in Inverness, wife of Alexander Ross in Gibraltar, died 9 May 1832. [Chapel Yard gravestone, Inverness]

INGLIS, JOHN, son of Hugh Inglis in Inverness, a merchant in Savanna, Georgia, was murdered in Charleston, South Carolina, on 8 April 1781. [Old High Church, Inverness, gravestone]

INGLIS, WILLIAM, of King's Mills, late Provost of Inverness, born 1747, died 4 February 1801. [Old High Church, Inverness]

IRVINE, JAMES, a horse thief, was sentenced at Inverness to transportation for fourteen years to the colonies in 1815. [NRS.GD1.959]

JACK, HUGH, born 1790, a cooper in Stuart Town, died on 23 March 1849. [Kirkton of Ardersier gravestone]

JAMIESON, ALEXANDER, a tenant on Keill, Canna, in 1848, 1851. [C.297/299]

JAMIESON, ALLAN, a tenant on Keill, Canna in 1848, 1851. [C.297/299]

JAMIESON, ANDREW, a tenant on Keill, Canna, in 1848, 1851, possibly emigrated to America. [C.297/299/302]

JAMIESON, CHARLES, a silversmith, was admitted as a burgess of Inverness in 1797. [Inverness Burgess Roll]

JAMIESON, CHARLES, son of Charles Jamieson a baillie and merchant in Inverness, a student at Marischal College, Aberdeen, in 1810. [MCA]

JAMIESON, EDWARD, tenant on Canna, 1818. [C.220]

JAMIESON, HUGH, tenant on Canna, 1818. [C.220]

JAMIESON, HUGH, son of Charles Jamieson a merchant in Inverness, was educated at Marischal College around 1808. [MCA]

JAMIESON, NIEL, tenant on Canna, 1818. [C.220]

JAMIESON, JOHN, tenant on Sanday, Canna, in 1818. [C.220]

JAMIESON, WILLIAM, sr., tenant on Canna, 1818. [C.220]

JAMIESON, WILLIAM, jr., tenant on Canna, 1818. [C.220]

JOASS, JAMES, from Inverness, graduated MA from King's College, Aberdeen, in March 1850, later a minister in Golspie. [KCA]

JOHNSTONE, JAMES, born in September 1777, son of James Johnstone and his wife Anne Fraser in Croy, [Crothaig], a farmer, with wife Mary born 1777 and son James born 1806, emigrated to New York aboard the George of New York in 1807. [TNA.PC1.3790]

JOHNSTONE, MARGARET, born 1767, a spinster from Croy, emigrated to New York aboard the George of New York in 1807. [TNA.PC1.3790]

JOHNSTONE, MARGARET, born 1737, a spinster in Croy, emigrated to New York aboard the George of New York in 1807. [TNA.PC1.3790]

KENNEDY, ALEXANDER, his wife, and two children, from Laddy, emigrated via Fort William aboard the Friends of Saltcoats master John How to Montreal in July 1802. [GkAd.59]

KENNEDY, DONALD, from Glen Urquhart, emigrated to Pictou, Nova Scotia, in 1801, settled on the East River. [TGS.53.451]

KENNEDY, DONALD, Angus Kennedy, Alexander Kennedy, Allan Kennedy with his wife and two children, from Inchlaggam, emigrated via Fort William aboard the Friends of Saltcoats master John How to Montreal in July 1802. [GkAd.59]

KENNEDY, DONALD, with four children from Kinlochlochy, emigrated via Fort William aboard the Friends of Saltcoats master John How to Montreal in July 1802. [GkAd.59]

KENNEDY, DONALD, from Glen Urquhart, emigrated to Pictou, Nova Scotia, in 1802, settled at Sunny Brae. [TGS.53.460]

KENNEDY, DONALD, with his wife, from Achluachrach, emigrated via Fort William aboard the Friends of Saltcoats master John How to Montreal in July 1802. [GkAd.59]

KENNEDY, DONALD, with his wife and two children, from Laddy, emigrated via Fort William aboard the Friends of Saltcoats master John How to Montreal in July 1802. [GkAd.59]

KENNEDY, DONALD, Margaret Kennedy, and three children, from Lewiston, emigrated via Fort William aboard the Friends of Saltcoats master John How to Montreal in July 1802. [GkAd.59]

KENNEDY, DONALD, third son of Angus Kennedy in Loanachen, a Member of the Legislative Council of Victoria, died in Melbourne, Australia, on 29 February 1864. [AJ.6072]

KENNEDY, EFFY, from Caum, emigrated via Fort William aboard the Friends of Saltcoats master John How to Montreal in July 1802. [GkAd.59]

KENNEDY, EWAN, with his wife, Peggy Kennedy, from Aberchalder, emigrated via Fort William aboard the Friends of Saltcoats master John How to Montreal in July 1802. [GkAd.59]

KENNEDY, EWAN, his wife, from Invergarry, [Inbhir Garadh], emigrated via Fort William aboard the Friends of Saltcoats master John How to Montreal in July 1802. [GkAd.59]

KENNEDY, FINLAY, in Glenbanchor, Kingussie, a victim of cattle stealing in 1837. [NRS.AD14.37.528]

KENNEDY, JOHN, with his wife, Duncan Kennedy, Alexander Kennedy, from Invervigar, emigrated via Fort William aboard the Friends of Saltcoats master John How to Montreal in July 1802. [GkAd.59]

KENNEDY, JOHN, with his wife, Ewen Kenned, Mary Kennedy, Alexander Kennedy, Janet Kennedy, Angus Kennedy, and 3 children, from Inchlaggan, [Innis an Lagain], emigrated via Fort William aboard the Friends of Saltcoats master John How to Montreal in July 1802. [GkAd.59]

KENNEDY, MARGARET, servant to John Dallas, in Cullernie, Petty, was accused of rioting at Croy Church in 1823. [NRS.AD14.23.235]

KENNEDY, MARY, from Laddy, emigrated via Fort William aboard the Friends of Saltcoats master John How to Montreal in July 1802. [GkAd.59]

KENNEDY, MARY, from Aberchalder, emigrated via Fort William aboard the Friends of Saltcoats master John How to Montreal in July 1802. [GkAd.59]

KERR, HENRY, born 1771 in Inverness, died in Charleston, South Carolina, on 1 January 1808. [Old Scots gravestone, Charleston]

KERR, HUGH, born 1771 in Inverness, died in Charleston, South Carolina, on 1 January 1808. [Old Scots gravestone, Charleston]

KER, JOHN CESSFORD, born 1779 in Inverness-shire, a merchant in Charleston, was naturalised in South Carolina on 20 January 1806. [NARA.M1183.1]

KINLOCH, LOCKHART, a writer in Inverness, son of William Kinloch a tailor in Nairn, was admitted as a Notary Public on 9 July 1795, sheriff clerk of Inverness from 1807, died on 16 May 1831. [NRS.NP2.35.261]

KINNAIRD, JOHN, born 1807, a shipmaster in Inverness, died 6 April 1867, husband of Agnes Fotheringham, born 1808, died 18 May 1888. [Chapel Yard gravestone, Inverness]

KYLE, JOHN, born 1820, son of James Kyle in Inverness, died in Berbice on 26 December 1845. [AJ.5120][Chapel Yard gravestone, Inverness]

LAMOND, DANIEL, born 1789, a piper of the 71st Highland Light Infantry for 27 years, he was present at the battles of Waterloo, Vittoria, Toulouse, Corunna, Walcheren, etc]

LAUGHLIN, ANDREW, acting Land Surveyor of the Customs at the Port of Inverness n 1820.   [NRS.E504.17.8]

LAWRENCE, JOHN, a shipowner in Inverness, died 11 April 1856, husband of Isabella Aitken who died on 25 April 1854. [Chapel Yard gravestone, Inverness]

LAWSON, LEWIS, in the Mains of Congash, Abernethy, testament, 19 March 1792, Comm. Inverness. [NRS]

LESLIE, CHARLES, from Inverness, failed to appear in court and]was fined one hundred merks Scots in 1819. [NRS.JC11.60]

LINDSAY, JOHN, of Bocard, Colin Lindsay a writer in Fort William, also Janet, Mary, and Jean Lindsay in Brocard, a petition in 1805. [NRS.CC2.7.52.12]

LINDSAY, Sergeant JOHN, of the Artillery, born 1741, died 22 April 1815, husband of Anne Campbell, born 1755, died 4 January 1818. [Kirkton of Ardersier gravestone]

LINDSAY, WILLIAM, born 1740 in Inverness, settled in America before 1760, a shipping merchant in Edenton, Chowan County, North Carolina, died 3 April 1817. [NCHGR.1.2] [Raleigh Register]

LILLIE, or STROTHER, MARGARET, in Petty, Inverness-shire, sister and heir of Jessie Lillie from Forres, Moray, later in Kingston, Jamaica, who died on 6 January 1832. [NRS.S/H]

LILLIE, MARY, in Inverness, sister and heir of Jessie Lillie from Forres, Moray, later in Kingston, Jamaica, who died on 6 January 1832. [NRS.S/H]

LIVINGSTONE, ALLAN, born 1781 in Lochaber, died 20 August 1854. [St David's gravestone, Antigonish, NS]

LOBAN, JOHN, born 1787, a carpenter in Daviot and Moy, died in April 1860, husband of Ann Vass, born 1790, died 21 December 1861. [Daviot gravestone]

LOGIE, ROBERT, with his wife Marjory Hay, and children Alexander born 1773, Margaret born 1775, William born 1778, and Patrick born 1780, from Bawds, Urquhart parish, settled in New Brunswick in 1780. [SG.23.171]

LYON, CATHERINE, wife of Reverend James Clark schoolmaster of Daviot, died there in 1836. [AJ.17.4.1836]

LYON, ROBERT, born 1790 in Inverness-shire, an agriculturalist, settled in the Swan River colony, Australia, 23 August 1829. [BPP.3.438/454]

MCALLISTER, CATHERINE, daughter of D D. MacAlister in Strathaird, Skye, married Livingstone Mitchell, eldest son of Lieutenant Colonel Sir Thomas Livingstone Mitchell of Parkhall, at Clifton, New South Wales, on 21 September 1847. [SG.1704]

MCALLISTER, RANALD, third son of Dr McAllister in Strathaird, Skye, died in Demerara on 31 March 1820. [BM.7.583]

MCALLISTER, SUSANNA, wife of Norman MacDonal of Scalpa, died in Inverness on 20 July 1820. [SM.86.192]S

MCALPIN, CATHERINE, from Letterfinlay, [Leitir Fhionnlaigh], emigrated via Fort William aboard the Friends of Saltcoats master John How to Montreal in July 1802. [GkAd.59][CMM]

MCALPIN, CATHERINE, from Aberchalder, emigrated via Fort William to Montreal in July 1802. [CMM]

MCALPIN, MARY, from Greenfield, emigrated via Fort William aboard the Friends of Saltcoats master John How to Montreal in July 1802. [GkAd.59] [CMM]

MCANDREW, JOHN, a victim of the riot at Croy Church in 1823. [NRS.AD14.23.35]

MACARTHUR, ALEXANDER, tenant on Canna, 1818. [C.220]

MACARTHUR, ALEXANDER, a tenant on Sanday, Canna, in 1848. [C.297]

MCARTHUR, ALEXANDER, sr., a tenant on Canna in 1851. [C.299]

MCARTHUR, ALEXANDER, a tenant on Canna in 1851. [C.299]

MCARTHUR, ALEXANDER, jr., a tenant on Canna in 1851. [C.299]

MACARTHUR, ALLAN, jr., tenant on Canna, 1818. [C.220]

MACARTHUR, ANGUS, a tenant on Sanday, Canna, in 1848. [C.297]

MCARTHUR, ARCHIBALD, a labourer from Kilmonivaig, with Christian, and an infant, emigrated via Fort William aboard the Sarah of Liverpool bound for Pictou, Nova Scotia, in June 1801. [NRS.RH2.4.87]

MCARTHUR, CHARLES, John McArthur, Sarah McArthur, Lizzie McArthur, Donald McArthur, from Inverskilroy, emigrated via Fort William aboard the Friends of Saltcoats master John How to Montreal in July 1802. [GkAd.59] [CMM]

MACARTHUR, CHARLES, tenant on Keill, Canna, 1848. [C.297]

MCARTHUR, DONALD, [1], a tenant on Canna in 1851. [C.299]

MCARTHUR, DONALD, [2], a tenant on Canna in 1851. [C.299]

MCARTHUR, DUNCAN, a tenant on Canna in 1851. [C.299]

MACARTHUR, FINLAY, tenant on Canna, 1818. [C.220]

MCARTHUR, FLORA, a tenant on Canna in 1851. [C.299]

MCARTHUR, JOHN, sr., tenant on Canna, 1818. [C.220]

MCARTHUR, JOHN, sr., tenant on Canna, 1818. [C.220]

MCARTHUR, JOHN, tenant on Keill, Canna, 1848. [C.297]

MCARTHUR, JOHN, a tenant on Canna in 1851. [C.299]

MACARTHUR, LACHLAN, tenant on Canna, 1818. [C.220]

MACARTHUR, LACHLAN, a tenant on Sanday, Canna, in 1848. [C.297]

MCARTHUR, LAUCHLAN, son of Peter McArthur a gamekeeper in Invereshie, Kingussie, was accused of maliciously attacking and invading inhabited dwellings in 1845. [NRS.AD14.4.122]

MACARTHUR, MALCOLM, tenant on Canna, 1818. [C.220]

MACARTHUR, MALCOLM, a tenant on Sanday, Canna, in 1818, 1848, 1851. [C.220/297/299]

MCARTHUR, PETER, born 1789 in Inverness, died in Judique, Nova Scotia, on 1 April 1831. [HJ.25.4.1831]

MCARTHUR, PETER, a gamekeeper, son of Peter McArthur a gamekeeper in Invereshie, Kingussie, was accused of maliciously attacking and invading inhabited dwellings in 1845. [NRS.AD14.4.122]

MACARTHUR, RONALD, a tenant on Sanday, Canna, in 1848. [C.297]

MCBAIN, LEWIS, in Kingussie, a sequestration petition in 1846. [NRS.CS279.1679]

MCBEAN, AENEAS, from Inverness, graduated MA from King's College, Aberdeen, on 31 March 1809, later a schoolmaster at Dores then a minister in Greenock. [KCA]

MCBEAN, AENEAS, jr., from Tomatin, a merchant in Glasgow, died on St Thomas, West Indies, in 1810. [EA.4873.167]

MCBEAN, ALEXANDER, a yeoman who emigrated to Canada and was granted land in Eldon, Newcastle, Upper Canada, on 8 March 1826. [PAO]

MCBEAN, ALEXANDER, born 1829, a town councillor of Inverness, died 23 October 1879, husband of Elizabeth Ross, born 1815, died 1870. [Old High gravestone, Inverness]

MCBEAN, Miss C. H., only child of Aeneas McBean of Tomatin and St Thomas, Danish West Indies, married Lieutenant Colonel of the 4th Royal Dragoon Guards, in Inverness on 7 April 1819. [EA.5778.233]

MCBEAN, DONALD, from Inverness, graduated MA from King's College, Aberdeen, on 30 March 1804, later a schoolmaster in Thurso. [KCA]

MCBEAN, Reverend FRANCIS, in Fort Augustus, a petition, 1845. [NRS.GD1.2.51.178]

MCBEAN, HUGH, from Inverness, graduated MA from King's College, Aberdeen, on 30 March 1807, later minister at Ardclach. [KCA]

MCBEAN, ANGUS, in Dores, died in August 1838, husband of Margaret McIntosh who died in August 1849. [Dores gravestone]

MCBEAN, JOHN, from Inverness, graduated MA from King's College, Aberdeen, on 26 April 1813. [KCA]

MACBEAN, JOHN GORDON, born 20 November 1797 in Inverness, son of Robert MacBean of Nairnside and his wife Margaret MacIntosh, a Captain of the 52nd Bengal Native Infantry, died in Chittagong, India, on 14 June 1828. [BA.3.110]

MCBEAN, NEIL, born 1753 in Inverness-shire, died in St Stephen, New Brunswick, on 18 June 1848. [QCG]

MCBEAN, ROBERT, from Tortula, West Indies, married Margaret McIntosh, daughter of McIntosh of Dalmagavie, in Inverness on 13 December 1794. [SM.56.801]

MCBEAN, WILLIAM, was granted a tack of Shenachie, Strathnairn, for nineteen years in 1839. [NRS.GD176.1453]

MCBEATH, Dr WILLIAM, born 25 February 1764 in Inverness, a physician in Demerara, died on 11 October 1797. [Chapel Yard gravestone, Inverness]

MCBEAN, WILLIAM, born 1768, weaver in Crook of Campbelltown, died 20 May 1839, husband of Isabella Urquhart, born 1774, died 24 March 1849. [Brachlich gravestone]

MCCALLUM, JOHN, born 1755, master gunner at Fort George, died 29 May 1833, husband of Christian Reid, born 1758, died 6 April 1813. [Kirkton of Ardersier gravestone]

MACCALLUM, MARGARET, a prisoner in Inverness Tolbooth accused of theft, was banished from Scotland for life in 1806. [NRS.JC11.48]

MCCALLUM, WILLIAM, settled in Philadelphia before 1864, son of Alexander McCallum, a farmer and distiller at Drumriach, Aird, who died in January 1849, brother of Alexander McCallum and of Hugh McCallum, MA, schoolmaster of Kirkhill. [Old High Church gravestone, Inverness]

MACCARMIC, JOHN, tenant on Canna, 1818. [C.220]

MACCARMIC, P., tenant on Canna, 1818. [C.220]

MCCASKILL, DONALD, grass-keeper to Reverend William Beatson in Divinish, Skye, guilty of cow stealing, was sentenced to transportation, at Inverness on 28 September 1785. [AJ.1970]

MACCASKILL, FINLAY, tenant on Canna, 1818. [C.220]

MCCASKILL, HECTOR, from Inverness, graduated MA from King's College, Aberdeen, on 30 March 1801. [KCA]

MCCASKILL, JOHN, born 1812, wife Catherine born 1826, daughter Mary born 1845, son John born 1848, and daughter Catherine born 1850, from Strathard, emigrated via Liverpool aboard the Priscilla bound for Victoria, Australia, on 15 October 1852. [NRS.HD4/5]

MCCASKILL, MALCOLM, from Inverness, graduated MA from King's College, Aberdeen, in March 1829. [KCA]

74

MCCASKILL, MARION, born 1824, in Horneval, Skye, emigrated via Liverpool aboard the Allison bound for Melbourne, Australia, on 13 September 1852. [NRS.HD4/5]

MCCASKILL, RACHEL, born 1839, from Portree, Skye, emigrated via Liverpool aboard the Priscilla bound for Victoria, Australia, on 15 October 1852. [NRS.HD4/5].

MCCAULEY, JAMES JOHN, an officer of the Revenue, who was obstructed at Strone, Kingussie, in 1823. [NRS.JC26.1823.12]

MCCLARRAN, Dr JOHN, born 1763, assistant surgeon of Fort George, died 13 December 1796. [Kirkton of Ardersier gravestone]

MCCOLE, DONALD, factor on the estates of Badenoch and Kincardine in 1815. [NRS.GD44.51.21.4]

MCCORQUODALE, JOHN, and his wife Margaret Mackenzie in Kiltarlity, parents of John McCorquodale, born in 1872, was]drowned in the Willamet River, Oregon, in 1892. [Tomnacross gravestone

MCCOWAN, MURDOCH, born 1841 in Inverness, was buried on 10 May 1913 in Katanning, Western Australia. [Katanning gravestone]

MCCRIMMON, ARCHIBALD, son of John McCrimmon in Glenelg, was accused of assault in 1824. [NRS.AD14.24.87]

MCCRIMMON, DONALD, son of Duncan McCrimmon a weaver in Glenelg, was accused of assault in 1824. [NRS.AD14.24.87]

MCCUAIGE, PETER, in Glen Elg, [Gleann Eilg], near Fort Augustus, applied to settle in Canada on 22 February 1819. [TNA.CO384.5.43]

MCCUAN, ANGUS, born 1803, wife Sarah born 1812, son Donald born 1833, son John born 1835, daughter Christy born 1837, son Murdoch born 1839, daughter Ann born 1843, and daughter Flora born 1845, from Herbusta, Skye, emigrated via Liverpool aboard the Priscilla bound for Victoria, Australia, on 15 October 1852. [NRS.HD4/5]

MCCULLOCH, JOHN, born 1756, a flax dresser in Inverness, died 12 August 1832, husband of Margaret McDonald, born 1770, died 17 January 1843, parents of Alexander McCulloch, born 1792, a draper in Inverness, died on 14 March 1848. [Old High Church gravestone, Inverness]

MCCULLOCH, JOHN, a wood merchant in Kingussie, 1812. [NRS.CS233.SEQN.M2.9]

MCCULLOCH, WILLIAM, born 1803, a gardener in Flemington, Ardesier, died 9 March 1865, husband of Catherine MacDonald, born 1820, died on Ingliston Muir on 10 April 1875, parents of John McCulloch a mason in Warwick, Queensland, Australia. [Wardlaw gravestone]

MCDIARMID, DONALD, born 1828, with Malcolm born 1839, from Stein, Skeabost, Skye, emigrated via Plymouth to Van Diemen's Land, [Tasmania], Australia, aboard the Louisa on 24 August 1852. [NRS.HD4/5]

MCDONALD, ALEXANDER, son of Duncan McDonald in Achnababaine, Glen Urquhart, emigrated to Nova Scotia on the Sarah in 1801, settled at Sunny Brae. [TGS.53.459]

MCDONALD, ALEXANDER, a tenant in Kilmorack, with Ann, Alexander born 1793], and John [born 197], emigrated via Fort William aboard the Sarah of Liverpool bound for Pictou, Nova Scotia, in June 1801. [NRS.RH2.4.87]

MACDONALD, ALEXANDER, in Crochill, Kiltarlity, guilty of stealing sheep, sentenced to transportation for fourteen years in 1810. [NRS.JC11.51]

76

MACDONALD, ALEXANDER, son of Angus MacDonald of Bohuntin, [Both Fhionndain], with his wife Mary Campbell and son Allan, emigrated to Nova Scotia in 1816. [CD.3.428]

MCDONALD, ALEXANDER, of Arnabie, and his wife Anne McDonald, settled in Canada before 1814. [CD.3.346]

MACDONALD, ALEXANDER, son of John MacDonald of Borrodale, a student at Marischal College, Aberdeen, in 1820s. [MCA]

MCDONALD, ALEXANDER, born 1804, his wife Mary born 1817, son John born 1839, daughter Margaret born 1841, daughter Ann born 1844, daughter Mary born 1847, and daughter Kate born 1851, from Kinlochmoidart, emigrated via Liverpool aboard the Allison bound for Melbourne, Australia, on 13 September 1852. [NRS.HD4/5]

MCDONALD, ALEXANDER, born 1818, his wife Flora born 1819, daughter Mary born 1844, daughter Catherine born 1848, and son Angus born 1850, from Kinlochmoidart, emigrated via Liverpool aboard the Allison bound for Melbourne, Australia, on 13 September 1852. [NRS.HD4/5]

MCDONALD, ALEXANDER, in Dundreggan, Urquhart, was murdered in 1829. [NRS.AD29.348]

MACDONALD, ALEXANDER, and John MacDonald, son of the late Donald MacDonald, a decreet of removal from Urchar Tollie and Dallinderg, Kilmonivaig, in 1808. [NRS.GD176.973]

MCDONALD, ALEXANDER, born 1798, a blacksmith in Dores, died 23 November 1834, husband of Elisabeth McIntosh. [Dores gravestone]

MCDONALD, ALEXANDER, born 1808, his wife Mary born 1809, son Alexander born 1834, son John born 1837, son Allan born 1839, daughter Ann born 1841, daughter Kate born 1844, and son Donald born 1847, from Kinlochmoidart, emigrated via Liverpool aboard the Allison bound for Melbourne, Australia, on 13 September 1852. [NRS.HD4/5]

MACDONALD, Mrs ALEXANDER, tenant on Canna, 1818. [C.220]

MCDONALD, ALLAN, a labourer from Knoydart [Cnoidart], Donald born 1791, Samuel born 1795, Peggy born 1797, and Mary born 1799, emigrated via Fort William on board the Sarah of Liverpool bound for Pictou, Nova Scotia, in 1801. [NRS.RH2.4.87/66-71]

MCDONALD, ALLAN, on Prince Edward Island, heir to his cousin John, son of Allan More MacDonald of Morar in 1825. [NRS.S/H]

MCDONALD, ANDREW, a merchant in Arisaig, emigrated in 1806, settled on Panmure Island, Prince Edward Island, Canada. [SCA]

MCDONALD, ANGUS, with his family of seven, emigrated from Druimdarroch on board the Jane bound for Prince Edward Island in 1790. [SCA]

MCDONALD, ANGUS, a farmer from Knoydart, with Margaret, Mary, Allan a labourer, Donald [born 1791], Samuel [born 1795], Peggy [born 1797], Mary [born 1799], emigrated via Fort William aboard the Sarah of Liverpool bound for Pictou, Nova Scotia, in June 1801. [NRS.RH2.4.87]

MCDONALD, ANGUS, a farmer from Knoydart, Margaret McDonald, a spinner, emigrated via Fort William on board the Sarah of Liverpool, bound for Pictou, Nova Scotia, in 1801. [NRS.RH2.4.87/66-71]

MCDONALD, ANGUS, a labourer from Glen Garry, with Janet, Rachel, Janet [born 1798], and Katherine, emigrated via Fort William aboard the Sarah of Liverpool bound for Pictou, Nova Scotia, in June 1801. [NRS.RH2.4.87]

MCDONALD, ANGUS, sr., born 1755 in Glenroy, Lochaber, emigrated to New Brunswick in 1805, died in St Andrews, New Brunswick, on 4 January 1830. [New Brunswick Royal Gazette.27.1.1830]

MACDONALD, ANGUS, a tenant on Canna in 1851. [C.299]

MCDONALD, ANGUS, born 1797, his wife Mary born 1804, and son Angus born 1850, from Kinlochmoidart, emigrated via Liverpool aboard the Allison bound for Melbourne, Australia, on 13 September 1852. [NRS.HD4/5]

MACDONALD, Mrs ANN, tenant on Sanday, Canna, in 1818. [C.220]

MACDONALD, ANTHONY, born 1770, Roman Catholic priest on Canna from 1791 until 1834, died on Eigg in 1843. [C.226]

MCDONALD, ARCHIBALD DOW, in Invercemore, Knoydart, was accused of perjury in 1806. [NRS.JC11.48]

MCDONALD, ARCHIBALD, shepherd to John Chisholm in Blairy, Glenmoriston, was accused of stealing sheep in 1821. [NRS.AD14.21.15]

MCDONALD, ARCHIBALD G., in Moy and Inverlair, a sequestration petition in 1845. [NRS.CS279.1785]

MCDONALD, CATHERINE, born 1757, died 20 December 1840, mother-in-law of James Bisset. [Dores gravestone]

MCDONALD, Mrs CATHERINE, born 1794 in Lochaber, died in Nova Scotia in 1865. [Merigomish gravestone, N.S.]

MCDONALD, CHARLES, born 1759 in Inverness, a mariner in Halifax, Nova Scotia, died 5 April 1789, probate 1789, Halifax, N.S.

MCDONALD, CHARLES, born 1843, son of Alexander McDonald and his wife Margaret Grant, died in Pietermaritzburg, South Africa, on 16 March 1880. [Duthil gravestone]

MACDONALD, CHRISTIAN, tenant on Canna, 1818. [C.220]

MCDONALD, COLIN, master of the Jean of Inverness trading with Ballachulish in 1822. [NRS.E504.17.9]

MCDONALD, DONALD, born 1742 in Glengarry, emigrated to New York in 1772, a Loyalist soldier during the War of Independence, died on Wolfe Island, Kingston, Upper Canada, on 18 September 1839. [New Brunswick Courier, 12 October 1839]

MCDONALD, DONALD, brother of Colonel McDonald of Kinlochmoidart, died in Banks, St Anne, Jamaica on 20 August 1794. [SM.56.734] [GM.64.1054]

MCDONALD, DONALD, a writer in Edinburgh, son of John McDonald the sheriff substitute of Inverness-shire, was admitted as a Notary Public on 1 June 1797. [NRS.NP2.36.93]

MCDONALD, DONALD, a labourer from Urquhart, emigrated via Fort William aboard the Sarah of Liverpool bound for Pictou, Nova Scotia, in June 1801. [NRS.RH2.4.87]

MCDONALD, DONALD, a farmer from Kiltarlity, emigrated via Fort William aboard the Sarah of Liverpool bound for Pictou, Nova Scotia, in June 1801. [NRS.RH2.4.87]

MCDONALD, Dr DONALD, in Fort Augustus, a letter to Sir Aeneas McIntosh in 1803. [NRS.GD176.2127]

MCDONALD, DONALD, born 1766 in Inverness-shire, died in Lochiel, Canada on 6 October 1850. [Quebec City Gazette]

MCDONALD, DONALD, his wife, and two children, from Inchlagan, emigrated via Fort William aboard the Friends of Saltcoats master John How to Montreal in July 1802. [GkAd.59]

MCDONALD, DONALD, son of Alexander McDonald and his wife Margaret in Glen Urquhart, emigrated to Nova Scotia in 1803, settled at Sunny Brae. [TGS.53.457]

MCDONALD, DONALD, a grocer in Inverness, 1812. [NRS.CS36.4.91]

MCDONALD, DONALD, was found guilty of stealing three cows in Inverness and sentenced to transportation to the colonies for fourteen years in 1815. [NRS.GD1.959]

MCDONALD, DONALD, born 29 October 1813 son of Allan McDonald a wheelwright and his wife Grace Shaw in Inverness, graduated MA from King's College, Aberdeen, in March 1830, later a minister in Inverness from 1842 until his death on 28 April 1892, husband of Ann Marjory Rose, parents of several children including, Alexander Rose McDonald who emigrated to Queensland, Australia. [F.6.459] [KCA]

MCDONALD, DONALD, in Uchnachan, Kilmonivaig, a victim of theft in 1824. [NRS.AD14.24.84]

MCDONALD, DONALD, from Inverness, graduated MA from King's College, Aberdeen, in March 1839, later minister of the Free Church in Edinkillie. [KCA]

MCDONALD, DONALD, son of John McDonald a shoemaker in Inverness, a student at Marischal College, Aberdeen, in 1850s. [MCA]

MACDONALD, DONALD, a tenant on Canna in 1851. [C.299]

MCDONALD, DUNCAN, from Cuderish, Kiltarlity, [Cill Targhlain], emigrated to Nova Scotia in 1801, settled at Sunny Brae. [TGS.53.458]

MCDONALD, DUNCAN, a labourer from Urquhart, with Janet, emigrated via Fort William aboard the Sarah of Liverpool bound for Pictou, Nova Scotia, in June 1801. [NRS.RH2.4.87]

MCDONALD, DUNCAN, a tenant in Kilmorack, with Isobel, Hugh [born 1798], and an infant, emigrated via Fort William aboard the Sarah of Liverpool bound for Pictou, Nova Scotia, in June 1801. [NRS.RH2.4.87]

MCDONALD, DUNCAN, a farmer from Kilmorack, with Janet, emigrated via Fort William aboard the Sarah of Liverpool bound for Pictou, Nova Scotia, in June 1801. [NRS.RH2.4.87]

MCDONALD, DUNCAN, a farmer in Urquhart, with Isobel, Mary [born 1796], John [born 1799], emigrated via Fort William aboard the Sarah of Liverpool bound for Pictou, Nova Scotia, in June 1801. [NRS.RH2.4.87]

MCDONALD, DUNCAN, from Glen Urquhart, father of John, settled at Sunny Brae, Nova Scotia, in 1801. [TGS.53.457]

MCDONALD, DUNCAN, born 1807, a farm servant in Dundreggan, Urquhart, was accused of culpable homicide in 1829. [NRS.AD14.29.348]

MCDONALD, DUNCAN, born 1827, died at Loch Flemington on 14 September 1907. [Brachlich gravestone]

MCDONALD, EWEN, a labourer from Strathglass, emigrated via Fort William aboard the Sarah of Liverpool bound for Pictou, Nova Scotia, in June 1801. [NRS.RH2.4.87]

MCDONALD, FARQUHAR, Land Surveyor of the Customs at the Port of Inverness in 1814.   [NRS.E504.17.8]

MCDONALD, FINLAY, a farmer from Urquhart, with Ann, John [born 1788], Ann [born 1791], Donald [born 1795], Christian [born 1797], and Duncan born 1800, emigrated via Fort William aboard the Sarah of Liverpool bound for Pictou, Nova Scotia, in June 1801. [NRS.RH2.4.87]

MCDONALD, FINLAY, was accused of assaulting Kenneth McLennon from Fort William and Robert Urquhart from Fort Augustus, Revenue Officers, in Boleskine and Abertarff, in 1823, was outlawed. [NRS.JC26.1823.14]

MCDONALD, FINLAY, son of the deceased William McDonald tenant of Balbeg of Bunlat in Urquhart, a deed 1831. [NRS.GD23.4.271]

MCDONALD, GILBERT, a blacksmith in Glen Urquhart, with his wife Mary McDonald, and son Donald born 1816, emigrated to Nova Scotia in 1821. [TGS.53.459]

MCDONALD, HUGH, tailor in Stratherrick, testament 8 February 1791, Comm. Inverness. [NRS]

MCDONALD, HUGH, a tenant in Moidart, Ann McDonald a spinner, a son born 1797, a son born 1799, emigrated via Fort William on board the Dove of Aberdeen bound for Pictou, Nova Scotia, in 1801. [NRS.RH2.4.87.75-5]

MCDONALD, HUGH, a cartwright at the Gate of Kilvarock, Croy, was accused of rioting at Croy Church in 1823. [NRS.AD14.23.235]

MCDONALD, HUGH, born 1806 in Inverness-shire, emigrated via Greenock to New York in 1826, petitioned to be naturalised in Marlboro, South Carolina, on 13 March 1833. [SCA]

MACDONALD, HUGH, tenant on Keill, Canna, 1848. [C.297]

MCDONALD, JAMES, born 1766 at Culloden, died in Savanna, Georgia, on 10 September 1811. [Savanna Republican. 12.9.1811]

MCDONALD, JAMES, a blacksmith from Fort Augustus, emigrated via Stromness on the Prince of Wales to the Hudson Bay Company settlement at Fort Churchill on 29 June 1813. [PAC.M155.165-8]

MACDONALD, JAMES, born 1804 in Lochaber, died 11 October 1850, his wife Mary, died 1850. [Mabou gravestone, Inverness County, NS]

MCDONALD, JANET, with Christian, from Kilmorack, emigrated via Fort William aboard the Sarah of Liverpool bound for Pictou, Nova Scotia, in June 1801. [NRS.RH2.4.87]

MCDONALD, JOHN, born 1746 in Inverness-shire, 'the last of the 500 respectable Highlanders who emigrated to Canada in 1784', died in Glengarry, Upper Canada, on 7 August 1836. [Weekly Chronicle, 23.9.1836] [S.1772] [AJ.4641]

MCDONALD, JOHN, a labourer from Kiltarlity, emigrated via Fort William aboard the Sarah of Liverpool bound for Pictou, Nova Scotia, in June 1801. [NRS.RH2.4.87]

MCDONALD, JOHN, with his family of three from Ardnish, Arisaig emigrated from Druimdarroch on board the Jane bound for Prince Edward Island in 1790. [SCA]

MCDONALD, JOHN, a farmer from Glenmoriston, emigrated via Fort William aboard the Sarah of Liverpool bound for Pictou, Nova Scotia, in June 1801. [NRS.RH2.4.87]

MCDONALD, JOHN, a farmer from Urquhart, with Elizabeth, Duncan [born 1795], Janet [born 1798], emigrated via Fort William aboard the Sarah of Liverpool bound for Pictou, Nova Scotia, in June 1801. [NRS.RH2.4.87]

MCDONALD, JOHN, son of John McDonald a pensioner, was accused of assaulting Kenneth McLennon from Fort William and Robert Urquhart from Fort Augustus, Revenue Officers, in Boleskine and Abertarff, in 1823, was outlawed. [NRS.JC26.1823.14]

MCDONALD, JOHN, with family of three, from Ardnish, [Aird Nis], Arisaig, emigrated via Druimindarroch, [Druim an Darach], on board the Jane bound for Prince Edward Island in July 1790. [PAPEI]

MCDONALD, JOHN, born 1768 in Moidart, died 12 August 1841. [Long Point Pioneer gravestone, Inverness County, NS]

MCDONALD, JOHN, born 1791 in Milton, Inverness-shire, died 1858, husband of Mary, ..., born 1793, died 1857. [Wallace gravestone, Cumberland County, NS]

MCDONALD, JOHN, a farmer in Moidart, Catherine McDonald, and a girl born 1800, emigrated via Fort William on board the Dove of Aberdeen bound for Pictou, Nova Scotia, in 1801. [NRS.RH2.4.87.75-5]

MCDONALD, JOHN, a farmer in Moidart, Catherine McDonald a spinner, Peggy McDonald born 1787, Catherine McDonald born 1792, Janet McDonald born 1795, Mary McDonald born 1798, emigrated via Fort William on board the Dove of Aberdeen bound for Pictou, Nova Scotia, in 1801. [NRS.RH2.4.87.75-5]

MCDONALD, JOHN, a labourer, Marian McDonald a spinner, Alexander McDonald born 1783, and an infant, emigrated via Fort William on board the Dove of Aberdeen bound for Pictou, Nova Scotia, in 1801. [NRS.RH2.4.87.75-5]

MCDONALD, JOHN, a tenant in Arisaig, Mary McDonald a spinner, emigrated via Fort William on board the Dove of Aberdeen bound for Pictou, Nova Scotia, in 1801. [NRS.RH2.4.87.75-5]

MCDONALD, JOHN, and his wife Elizabeth Grant, from Glen Urquhart, settled at Sunny Brae, Nova Scotia, in 1801. [THS.53.458]

MCDONALD, JOHN, with his wife, from Inchlaggan, [Innis na Lagain], emigrated via Fort William aboard the Friends of Saltcoats master John How to Montreal in July 1802. [GkAd.59]

MCDONALD, JOHN, his wife, Alexander McDonald, Donald McDonald, Peggy McDonald, from Kinlochnasale, emigrated via Fort William aboard the Friends of Saltcoats master John How to Montreal in July 1802. [GkAd.59]

MCDONALD, JOHN, from Doers, [Dubhras], emigrated via Fort William aboard the Friends of Saltcoats master John How to Montreal in July 1802. [GkAd.59]

MACDONALD, JOHN, tenant of Keninellan, Canna, in 1813-1815 [C.219]

MACDONALD, JOHN, son of Alexander MacDonald of Drimindarach, a surgeon on South Uist, emigrated to America in 1824. [CD]

MCDONALD, JOHN, a schoolmaster in Arisaig, a letter, 24 March 1808. [NRS.NRAS.2177, bundle 1532]

MCDONALD, JOHN, imprisoned in Inverness Tolbooth, found guilty of stealing horses, was sentenced to fourteen years transportation in 1815. [NRS.JC26.1815.60]

MCDONALD, JOHN, from Arisaig, emigrated via Tobermory, [Tobar Mhoire], on board the Emperor Alexander of Aberdeen bound for Sydney, Cape Breton, in July 1823, landed there on 16 September 1823. [Inverness Journal, 30 January 1824]

MACDONALD, JOHN, son of Allan More MacDonald of Morar, dead by 1825, cousin of Allan MacDonald on Prince Edward Island. [NRS.S/H]

MACDONALD, JOHN, born 1820, farmer in Tirfochrein, Croy, died 15 April 1893. [Brachlich gravestone]

MACDONALD, JOHN, [1822-1903], a farmer in Beauly, husband of Marjory Douglas, [1830-1903], parents of James MacDonald, born 1862, died in Los Angeles, California, on 15 May 1893. [Old Kilmorack gravestone]

MCDONALD, JOHN, from Inverness, graduated MA from King's College, Aberdeen, in March 1826. [KCA]

MCDONALD, JOHN, a crofter on the Moor of Petty, was alleged to have used abusive and threatening conduct to Alexander Campbell the minister of Croy in 1831. [NRS.GD23.6.669]

MCDONALD, JOHN, a ship carpenter in Clachnaharry, husband of Isobel Corbet who died on 15 February 1808. [Kirkton of Bunchrew gravestone]

MCDONALD, JOHN, was accused of a murder at Lochy Ferry, Kilmonivaig, in 1846, found guilty and sentenced to eighteen months in Perth prison. [NRS.JC26.1846.1]

MACDONALD, JOHN, in Scothouse, Knoydart, dead by 1853, grandfather of John MacDonald in Sandy Point, Canada. [NRS.S/H]

MCDONALD, JOHN, from Inverness, graduated MA from King's College, Aberdeen, in March 1843, later minister of the Free Church in Clyne. [KCA]

MACDONALD, JOHN, a tenant on Canna in 1851, possibly emigrated to America. [C.299/302]

MCDONALD, JOHN, a farmer in Beauly, [1822-1903] and his wife Marjory Douglas, [1830-1903], parents of James McDonald, born 1862, died in Los Angeles, California, on 15 May 1893. [Kilmorack Old Parish gravestone]

MACDONALD, KATHERINE, a spinner from Arisaig, emigrated via Fort William on board the Dove of Aberdeen bound for Pictou, Nova Scotia, in 1801. [NRS.RH2.4.87.75-5]

MCDONALD, LAUCHLAN, a tenant in Moidart, Catherine McDonell, a girl born 1798, and an infant, emigrated via Fort William on board the Dove of Aberdeen bound for Pictou, Nova Scotia, in 1801. [NRS.RH2.4.87.75-5]

MCDONALD, MARGARET, in Muckcoul, Laggan, a victim of theft in 1835. [NRS.AD.14.35.4]

MCDONALD, MARY and MARGARET, in Garth of Strathnairn, Daviot, victims of housebreaking and theft in 1837. [NRS.AD14.37.3]

MCDONALD, PATRICK, a labourer from Urquhart, emigrated via Fort William aboard the Sarah of Liverpool bound for Pictou, Nova Scotia, in June 1801. [NRS.RH2.4.87]

MCDONALD, PAUL, a farmer from Urquhart, with Ann, John [born 1791], Donald [born 1793], Margaret [born 1795], Alexander [born 1797], emigrated via Fort William aboard the Sarah of Liverpool bound for Pictou, Nova Scotia, in June 1801. [NRS.RH2.4.87]

MCDONALD, RANALD, a farmer from Arisaig, with John born 1795, and Janet born 1798, emigrated via Fort William on board the Dove of Aberdeen bound for Pictou, Nova Scotia, in 1801. [NRS.RH2.4.87.75-5]

MCDONALD, Captain RANALD, in Forlundy, Kilmonivaig, victim of assault in 1836. [NRS.AD14.36.43; JC26.1836.109]

MACDONALD, RANALD, in Girinish, Canada, nephew and heir of his uncle Allan MacDonald on Prince Edward Island, 1853, also, cousin and heir of Major Simon MacDonald of Morar, 2 August 1854. [NRS.S/H]

MCDONALD, RODERICK, a tenant farmer from Glenuig [Gleann Uige], with five of a family, emigrated via Druimindarroch on board the Jane bound for Prince Edward Island in July 1790. [PAPEI][SCA]

MCDONALD, RODERICK, a skin merchant and convenor of the six incorporated trades of Inverness, husband of Janet MacDonald, born 1753, died 12 September 1810. [Old High gravestone, Inverness]

MCDONALD, RONALD GEORGE, of Clan Ranald, 1813. [NRS.GD201.5.281]

MCDONALD, RORY, a tenant in Urquhart, with Mary, Catherine, Janet [born 1796], emigrated via Fort William aboard the Sarah of Liverpool bound for Pictou, Nova Scotia, in June 1801. [NRS.RH2.4.87]

MCDONALD, RORY, a labourer from Kilmorack, with Catherine, emigrated via Fort William aboard the Sarah of Liverpool bound for Pictou, Nova Scotia, in June 1801. [NRS.RH2.4.87]

MACDONALD, RORY, a tenant on Canna in 1851. [C.299]

MACDONALD, Lieutenant SOIRLE, born 1724, died in Kilmuir in 1830. [AJ.10.10.1830]

MCDONALD, SWEEN, born 1742, a boat-builder in Clachnaharry, died 15 July 1828, husband of Janet McKay, born 1739, died 1811. [Kirkton of Bunchrew gravestone]

MCDONALD, THOMAS, a labourer from Kilmorack, with Janet, emigrated via Fort William aboard the Sarah of Liverpool bound for Pictou, Nova Scotia, in June 1801. [NRS.RH2.4.87]

MCDONALD, WILLIAM, born 1763 in Inverness, of the Ordnance Department, died in Halifax, Nova Scotia, on 30 January 1838. [Acadian Recorder, 3.2.1838]

MCDONALD, WILLIAM, a labourer from Urquhart, emigrated via Fort William aboard the Sarah of Liverpool bound for Pictou, Nova Scotia, in June 1801. [NRS.RH2.4.87]

MCDONALD, WILLIAM, a farmer from Kiltarlity, with Janet, Mary [born 1788], Ann [born 1791], John [born 1793], Catherine [born 1796], Henry [born 1798], and an infant, emigrated via Fort William aboard the Sarah of Liverpool bound for Pictou, Nova Scotia, in June 1801. [NRS.RH2.4.87]

MCDONALD. WILLIAM, from Inverness, graduated MA from King's College, Aberdeen, in March 1850, later a schoolmaster in Broughty Ferry. [KCA]

MACDONELL, AENEAS, son of Aeneas MacDonell of Scothouse, graduated MA from Marischal College, Aberdeen, in 1807, later in the Service of the East India Company, the first member of the Madras Board of Revenue. [MCA]

MCDONELL, ALEXANDER, born 1760 in Inverness, Speaker of the House of the Assembly in Upper Canada, died in Toronto on 18 March 1842. [Weekly Chronicle,15.4.1842]

MCDONNELL, Captain ALEXANDER, late of the Glengarry Fencibles, from Fechem, Glengarry, died in Ellora, Canada West, on 22 January 1850. [W.XI.1113]

MCDONELL, ALEXANDER, with his wife and two children, from Laggan, [An Lagan], emigrated via Fort William aboard the Friends of Saltcoats master John How to Montreal in July 1802. [GkAd.59]

MCDONELL, ALEXANDER, Mary McDonell, and three children, from Munerigy, emigrated via Fort William aboard the Friends of Saltcoats master John How to Montreal in July 1802. [GkAd.59]

MCDONELL, ALEXANDER, his wife, Duncan McDonell, Donald McDonell, Catherine McDonell, and four children, from Boiyne, [Both Fhloinn], emigrated to Canada in 1802.

MCDONELL, ALLAN, with his wife, Catherine McDonell, Margaret McDonell, Donald McDonell, and two children from Munerigy, emigrated via Fort William aboard the Friends of Saltcoats master John How to Montreal in July 1802. [GkAd.59]

MCDONELL, ALLAN, born 1722 in Glengarry, Inverness-shire, died at Three Rivers, Quebec. [Halifax Journal, 26.11.1821]

MCDONELL, ANGUS, his wife, Duncan McDonell Katherine McDonell, Margaret McDonell, Alexander McDonell, and John

McDonell, from Invervigar, emigrated via Fort William aboard the Friends of Saltcoats master John How to Montreal in July 1802. [GkAd.59]

MCDONELL, ANGUS, tacksman of Crochell Strathglass, Kiltarlity, was accused of sheep stealing in 1818. [NRS.AD14.18.74]

MCDONELL, DONALD, his wife and three children, from Thornhill, emigrated via Fort William aboard the Friends of Saltcoats master John How to Montreal in July 1802. [GkAd.59]

MCDONELL, DONALD, with two children, from Inchlaggan, [Innis an Lagain], emigrated via Fort William aboard the Friends of Saltcoats master John How to Montreal in July 1802. [GkAd.59]

MCDONELL, DONALD, John McDonell, Duncan McDonell, Catherine McDonell, from Laddy, emigrated via Fort William aboard the Friends of Saltcoats master John How to Montreal in July 1802. [GkAd.59]

MCDONELL, DONALD, his wife, Mary McDonell, Janet McDonell, Janet McDonell, Catherine McDonell, Allan McDonell, and four children, from Inchlaggan, [Innis an Lagain], emigrated via Fort William aboard the Friends of Saltcoats master John How to Montreal in July 1802. [GkAd.59]

MCDONELL, DONALD, his wife, Anne McDonell, Duncan McDonell, Ewan McDonell, and 2 children, from Aberchalder, [Obar Chaladair], emigrated via Fort William aboard the Friends of Saltcoats master John How to Montreal in July 1802. [GkAd.59]

MCDONELL, DONALD, and his wife, from Leck, emigrated via Fort William aboard the Friends of Saltcoats master John How to Montreal in July 1802. [GkAd.59]

MCDONELL, ELIZABETH, eldest daughter of Colonel Ranald McDonell of Glengarry, wife of R. C. McDonald of the 30th Regiment, died in St John's, New Brunswick, on 22 December 1842. [AJ.4959][EEC.20554]

MACDONNELL, ENEAS RANALD, in Glengarry, trial in 1836. [NRS.JC11.84]

MACDONELL, GEORGE, born 20 March 1787 in Glen Elg, son of John MacDonell of Finiskaig, a Lieutenant of the 23rd Bengal Native Infantry, died in Calcutta, India, on 8 September 1818. [BA.3.128]

MACDONELL, G. B., Superintendent Surgeon in Madras, India, son of Alexander MacDonell of Milnfield, died on 10 April 1850 aboard the steamer Indus on passage from India to England, was buried in the Protestant cemetery in Malta. [Chapel Yard gravestone, Inverness]

MACDONELL, GEORGE BEAN, born 1840, son of G. B. Macdonell a surgeon in the Indian Army, a Colonel of the Royal Artillery, who died on 22 March 1896. [Chapel Yard gravestone, Inverness]

MCDONELL, JAMES, with his wife, Katherine McDonell, Allan McDonell, and four children, from Balmean, [Baile Meadhain], emigrated via Fort William aboard the Friends of Saltcoats master John How to Montreal in July 1802. [GkAd.59]

MACDONELL, JAMES, born 1787, a Writer to the Signet, died in Edinburgh on 23 November 1841. [Chapel Yard gravestone, Inverness]

MCDONELL, JOHN, born 1728, son of John McDonell of Crowlin, [Crolaigeach], and his wife Janet McLeod, settled at Inverguseran, [Inbhir Ghuiseirein], Moidart, emigrated to Canada on the Pearl in 1775, an officer of the 84th [Royal Highland Emigrants] Regiment during the American Revolution, moved to Canada, died in Cornwall, Upper Canada, on 15 April 1810. [CD][CR] on 16 August 1790. [PAC.RG4A1, VOL.48.PP15874-5]

MCDONELL, JOHN, Dugald McDonell, Catherine McDonell, Flory McDonell, Peggy McDonell, Donald McDonell, and one child, from Invervigar, emigrated via Fort William aboard the Friends of Saltcoats master John How to Montreal in July 1802. [GkAd.59]

MCDONELL, JOHN, from Leck, emigrated via Fort William aboard the Friends of Saltcoats master John How to Montreal in July 1802. [GkAd.59]

MCDONELL, JOHN, with wife and child, from Ardnabie, emigrated via Fort William aboard the Friends of Saltcoats master John How to Montreal in July 1802. [GkAd.59]

MCDONELL, JOHN, from Divach, [Diobhach], emigrated via Fort William aboard the Friends of Saltcoats master John How to Montreal in July 1802. [GkAd.59]

MCDONELL, MARGARET, with three children, from Aberchalder, emigrated via Fort William aboard the Friends of Saltcoats master John How to Montreal in July 1802. [GkAd.59]

MCDONELL, MARY, with five children, from Achluachrach, emigrated via Fort William aboard the Friends of Saltcoats master John How to Montreal in July 1802. [GkAd.59]

MCDONELL, MARY, from Kerrowdoun, [An Cearthramh Donn], emigrated via Fort William aboard the Friends of Saltcoats master John How to Montreal in July 1802. [GkAd.59]

MCDONELL, MILES, born 1767 in Inverness, settled in Tryon County, New York, a Loyalist, an officer of the Royal Canadian Volunteers, later in Hudson Bay Company Service from 1811 to 1820, died at Port Fortune on the Ottawa River, on 28 June 1828. [HBRS.2.232]

MCDONELL, RANALD, from Achteraw, [Uachdar Abha], emigrated via Fort William aboard the Friends of Saltcoats master John How to Montreal in July 1802. [GkAd.59]

MCDONELL, RONALD, a labourer in Reddwick, Glen Elg, accused of housebreaking and theft in 1843. [NRS.AD14.43.7]

MCDONELL, RODERICK, a labourer from Kiltarlity, with Ann McDonald, Catherine, Janet, John [born 1799], and a child, emigrated via Fort William aboard the Sarah of Liverpool bound for Pictou, Nova Scotia, in June 1801. [NRS.RH2.4.87]

MCDONELL, WILLIAM, a tenant in Strathglass, was accused of housebreaking and theft in 1814, found guilty and sentenced to seven years transportation beyond the seas. [NRS.JC26.1814.10]

MCDONELL, WILLIAM ALEXANDER, born 1782 in Inverness, former Speaker of the Upper House of Assembly in Canada, died in Toronto on 18 March 1842. [Weekly Chronicle, 15.4.1842]

MACDONNEL, WILLIAM, son of Aeneas MacDonnel of Scothouse, a student at Marischal College, Aberdeen, around 1809. [MCA]

MCDOUGALD, ANNE, from Knoydart, with Ereck, emigrated via Fort William aboard the Sarah of Liverpool bound for Pictou, Nova Scotia, in June 1801. [NRS.RH2.4.87]

MCDOUGALD, CATHERINE, a spinner in Arisaig, emigrated via Fort William on board the Dove of Aberdeen bound for Pictou, Nova Scotia, in 1801. [NRS.RH2.4.87.75]

MCDOUGALD, DONALD, with his wife, Marjery McDougald, Alexander McDougald, and John McDougald, from Fort Augustus, emigrated via Fort William aboard the Friends of Saltcoats master John How to Montreal in July 1802. [GkAd.59]

MACDOUGALL, ANGUS, tenant on Keill, Canna, 1848. [C.297]

MACDOUGALL, DUGALD, a tenant on Canna in 1851. [C.299]

MCDOUGALL, JOHN, born 15 March 1805, son of John McDougall and his wife Euphemia Bethune on Ailean Mor, Glen Urquhart, settled at Blue Mountain, Pictou, Nova Scotia, in 1828, died 1 July 1873. [TGS.53.445]

MCDOUGAL, CHARLES, from Inverness, graduated MA from King's College, Aberdeen, in March 1820. [KCA]

MCDOUGALL, DANIEL, born 1745 in Inverness-shire, died in Nova Scotia on 2 March 1831. [AR.12.3.1831]

MCDOUGALL, H., Ground officer of Canna, 1848. [Cc.297]

MCDOUGALL, JOHN, from Inverness, father of a daughter born in Montreal on 28 June 1846. [AJ.5142]

MCDOUGALL, RODERICK, and his wife Christy McMillan, in Allt Saithe, Glen Urquhart, settled at Blue Mountain, Pictou, Nova Scotia, in 1828, died 1854. [TGS.53.447]

MCDOWELL, Colonel, of Laggan, a petition for a redemption of land tax in 1817. [NRS.CS230.MC8.30]

MCFARLANE, ARCHIBALD, a farmer from Arisaig, emigrated via Fort William on board the Dove of Aberdeen bound for Pictou, Nova Scotia, in 1801. [NRS.RH2.4.87.75-5]

MCFARLANE, DOUGALD, a labourer from Arisaig, emigrated via Fort William on board the Dove of Aberdeen bound for Pictou, Nova Scotia, in 1801. [NRS.RH2.4.87.75-5]

MCFARLANE, HUGH FALCONER, born 15 January 1788, son of Andrew McFarlane, Episcopal Bishop of Moray, and his wife Magdalene Duff, a Lieutenant of the 3rd Bengal Native Infantry, died at Serampore, India, on 13 February 1817. [BA.3.131]

MCFARLANE, JOHN, a labourer from Arisaig, Peggy McFarlane born 1789, Angus McFarlane born 1794, emigrated via Fort William on board the Dove of Aberdeen bound for Pictou, Nova Scotia, in 1801. [NRS.RH2.4.87.75-5]

MACFARLANE, PEGGY, a spinner in Arisaig, emigrated via Fort William on board the Dove of Aberdeen bound for Pictou, Nova Scotia, in 1801. [NRS.RH2.4.87.75-5]

MCFARLANE, PETER, a labourer from Arisaig, emigrated via Fort William on board the Dove of Aberdeen bound for Pictou, Nova Scotia, in 1801. [NRS.RH2.4.87.75-5]

MCGILLIVRAY, ALEXANDER, born 1788, died 28 November 1874, husband of Nancy McLeod, both from Inverness-shire. [Caledonia gravestone, Pictou, NS]

MCGILLIVRAY, Colonel ALEXANDER, born in Drumnaglass, Chief of the Creeks, died in the Creek Territory in 1792. [SM.54.310]

MCGILLIVIRAY,....., son of Colonel Alexander McGillivray, died in Pensacola, West Florida, on 17 February 1793. [SM.55.413]

MCGILLIVRAY, ALEXANDER, in Daviot, son of Archibald McGillivray a merchant late of Charleston, South Carolina, a precept of clare constat by Aeneas Mackintosh of Mackintosh and his spouse Lucy Mackintosh, in 1806. [NRS.GD176.891/892] [a non extant document]

MCGILLIVRAY, ALEXANDER, born in Croy, son of Alexander McGillivray, was educated at King's College, Aberdeen, in 1827, a minister in Nova Scotia from 1833, died on 16 February 1862. [F.7.615]

MCGILLIVRAY, ANN, born 1773, widow of Donald McIntosh, died in Columbiana County, Ohio, on 4 February 1850. [Dalarossie gravestone]

MCGILLVRAY, ARCHIBALD, late merchant in Charleston, South Carolina, husband of Lucy Mackintosh, father of Alexander McGillvray in Daviot, and of James McGillvray late in Georgia, 1809. [NRS.GD176.891-895]

MCGILLIVRAY, CHARLES CALDER, son of Reverend D. McGillivray in Kilmalie, died in Grenada on 6 April 1845. [AJ.5082][W.567]

MCGILLIVRAY, DONALD, from Inverness, graduated MA from King's College, Aberdeen, on 28 March 1801, later minister at Lochgoilhead and Kilmalie. [KCA]

MCGILLIVRAY, FARQUHAR, of Dalcrombie, dead by 1852, father of John McGillivray in Glengarry, Canada. [NRS.S/H]

MCGILLIVRAY, JAMES, late of Savannah, Georgia, then in Inverness, probate, November 1806, PCC. [TNA]; [NRS.GD176.895]

MCGILLIVRAY, JAMES, a shoemaker from Inverness, with Mary McBean his wife, and family, emigrated to Canada in 1833, settled in Megantic County, Quebec. [AMC.48]

MCGILLVRAY, JOHN, with family of five, from Marney, Arisaig, emigrated via Driumindarroch, on board the Jane bound for Prince Edward Island in July 1790. [SCA]

MCGILLIVRAY, JOHN, was granted a tack of Little Mills, Strathnairn, for fourteen years in 1839. [NRS.GD176.1453]

MCGILLIVRAY, JOHN, of Dunmglass, died 6 February 1852, cousin of Neil John McGillivray in Canada West. [NRS.S/H]

MCGILLIVRAY, JOHN, in Glengarry, Canada, heir to Farquhar McGillivray of Dalcrombie, 1852. [NRS.S/H]

MCGILVRAY, MARY, from Kinlochnasale, emigrated via Fort William aboard the Friends of Saltcoats master John How to Montreal in July 1802. [GkAd.59]

MCGILLIVRAY, MARY, sister of William McGillivray of Argyll and Montreal, died in Elmwood, Montreal, on 28 April 1854. [GM.NS42.90]

MCGILLIVRAY, NEIL JOHN, in Canada West, heir to his remote cousin John McGillivray of Dunmaglass who died 6 February 1852. [NRS.S/H]

MCGILLIVRAY, SIMON, born 1783 in Inverness-shire, a merchant in Montreal by 1813. [HBRS.1.451]

MCGILLIVRAY, WILLIAM, was granted a tack of Balnacraig and Achbain, Strathnairn, for nineteen years in 1835. [NRS.GD176.1453]

MCGREGOR, ALEXANDER, a farmer from Urquhart, with Christian, William born 1798, emigrated via Fort William aboard the Sarah of Liverpool bound for Pictou, Nova Scotia, in June 1801. [NRS.RH2.4.87]

MCGREGOR, ALEXANDER, born 1793, from Strathglass, emigrated via Fort William aboard the Sarah of Liverpool bound for Pictou, Nova Scotia, in June 1801. [NRS.RH2.4.87]

MCGREGOR, ALEXANDER, from Inverness, graduated MA from King's College, Aberdeen, in March 1827, later a minister in Kilmuir, Edinburgh, and Inverness. [KCA]

MCGREGOR, DONALD, a farmer in Kiltarlity, with Isobel, Mary [born 1790], John [born 1792], Jean [born 1793], Alexander [born 1795], Andrew [born 1797], and Kate [born 1799], emigrated via Fort William aboard the Sarah of Liverpool bound for Pictou, Nova Scotia, in June 1801. [NRS.RH2.4.87]

MCGREGOR, DUNCAN, a merchant in Fort William, versus Ewan Kennedy, father of the deceased Alexander Kennedy in Strone, also Peter and Donald Kennedy brothers of the defunct, residing in Inverskilavulin, in 1805. [NRS.CC2.2.106.1]

MCGREGOR, DUNCAN, in Blarnachurich, Kilmally, a victim of cattle stealing in 1837. [NRS.AD14.37.528]

MCGREGOR, JOHN, born 1764, a weaver, died 29 May 1828, husband of Margaret Fraser, born 1765, died 6 January 1806, parents of Thomas MacGregor a baker and guilds-brother of Inverness. [Old High gravestone, Inverness]

MCGREGOR, RODERICK, born 1756, died 28 September 1828, husband of Helen Gordon. [Chapel Yard gravestone, Inverness]

MCGUIRMAN, DONALD, aged over 70 years, a farmer in Inverness, a deposition re Alexander Mackintosh of Mackintosh in 1820. [NRS.GD176.902]

MCGUIRMAN, THOMAS, born 12 September 1784 near Inverness, son of Donald McGuirman and his wife Elspet Kerr, was apprenticed to Alexander Stewart, a silversmith in Inverness, in 1798. [Inverness Hammermen's Minute Book]

MACINNES, ANGUS, a labourer in Arisaig, with Jean Macinnes born 1794, and Duncan Macinnes born 1796, emigrated via Fort William on board the Dove of Aberdeen bound for Pictou, Nova Scotia, in 1801. [NRS.RH2.4.87.75-5]

MCINNES, ANGUS, master of the Kitty and Lucy of Fort William trading with Inverness in 1807. [NRS.E504.17.8]

MCINNES, ANGUS, a tenant on Keill, Canna in 1848/1851. [C.297/299]

MACINNES, CATHERINE, a tenant in Arisaig, emigrated via Fort William on board the Dove of Aberdeen bound for Pictou, Nova Scotia, in 1801. [NRS.RH2.4.87.75-5]

MACINNES, DONALD, a tenant in Arisaig, emigrated via Fort William on board the Dove of Aberdeen bound for Pictou, Nova Scotia, in 1801. [NRS.RH2.4.87.75-5]

MCINNES, HUGH, tenant on Keill, Canna, 1848. [C.297]

MACINNES, JOHN, tenant on Canna, 1818. [C.220]

MCINNES, JOHN, born 1812 in Fort George, a soldier of the 42nd Regiment, accused of theft in Glasgow in 1837. [NRS.AD14.37.278]

MCINNES, NEIL, a tenant on Canna in 1851, possibly emigrated to America. [C.299/302]

MCINTOSH, A., born 1742 in Glengarry, and his wife C., born 1754 in Glengarry, emigrated to Canada in 1793, died at Martintown, Upper Canada, on 20 January 1834. [Free Press, 18.2.1834]

MCINTOSH, ALEXANDER, from Inverness, graduated MA from King's College, Aberdeen, on 30 March 1801. [KCA]

MCINTOSH, ALEXANDER, minister of the united parishes of Moy and Dalarossie in 1804. [NRS.GD1.187.18]

MCINTOSH, ALEXANDER, a farmer from Kilmorack, with Catherine, Janet, and Margaret, [born 1787], emigrated via Fort William aboard the Sarah of Liverpool bound for Pictou, Nova Scotia, in June 1801. [NRS.RH2.4.87]

MACINTOSH, ALEXANDER, born 1793, died at Balrobert on 18 August 1863, husband of Ann MacDonald, born 1801, died at Scaniport on 3 September 1876. [Dores gravestone]

MACINTOSH, ALEXANDER, was granted a tack of the lands of Coignafearn, Dalarossie, and the lands of Tomlias, Daviot, for eighteen years by The Mackintosh in 1805. [NRS.GD176.1437]

MCINTOSH, ALEXANDER, was granted a tack of Craskhemish, Strathnairn, for ten years in 1840. [NRS.GD176.1453]

MCINTOSH, ALLAN, from Inverness, graduated MA from King's College, Aberdeen, on 31 March 1827. [KCA]

MACKINTOSH, ANGUS, born 1790 in Inverness-shire, died 1819 in Beaufort, South Carolina. [Old Third Presbyterian gravestone, Charleston, S.C.]

MACKINTOSH, ANGUS, of Mackintosh, at Daviot, an inventory,1833. [NRS.GD176.1160]

MCINTOSH, ANGUS, was granted a tack of Beachain, Strathnairn, for nineteen years in 1843. [NRS.GD176.1453]

MACKINTOSH, ANN, sister of Angus Mackintosh of Olm, died 'at an advanced age' in Inverness on 30 May 1820. [SM.86.190]

MACKINTOSH, CAMPBELL, a writer in Inverness, factor of the Macintosh of Macintosh, 1798-1802. [NRS.GD176.1825]

MACINTOSH, CHARLES, born 1782, eldest son of Alexander MacIntosh and his wife Janet McLean, was drowned in the River Essequibo on 21 April 1814. [Greyfriars gravestone, Inverness]

MACINTOSH, DONALD, a writer in Edinburgh, son of William MacIntosh in Eilig, was admitted as a Notary Public on 4 February 1797. [NRS.NP2.36.49]

MCINTOSH, DONALD, born 1750, a farmer in Mobile, died in May 1825. [Dalarossie gravestone]

MCINTOSH, DONALD, a farmer from Urquhart, with Janet, and Isobel [born 1798], emigrated via Fort William aboard the Sarah of Liverpool bound for Pictou, Nova Scotia, in June 1801. [NRS.RH2.4.87]

MCINTOSH, DONALD, a farmer from Kilmorack, emigrated via Fort William aboard the Sarah of Liverpool bound for Pictou, Nova Scotia, in June 1801. [NRS.RH2.4.87]

MCINTOSH, DONALD, born 1788, the former British Consul in Maine, died in Inverness on 29 December 1845. [AJ.5116]

MCINTOSH, DONALD, a farmer from Glenelg, with Mary, Surmy [born 1789], Anne [born 1793], Donald [born 1796], and Mary [born 1798], emigrated via Fort William aboard the Sarah of Liverpool bound for Pictou, Nova Scotia, in June 1801. [NRS.RH2.4.87]

MCINTOSH, DONALD, born 4 July 1809 in Inverness-shire, settled in Charleston, South Carolina, naturalised there on 12 October 1830, died in S.C. on 16 July 1864. [NARA.M1183.1] [Old Third Presbyterian gravestone, Charleston]

MACINTOSH, DONALD, tenant on Canna, 1818. [C.220]

MCINTOSH, DONALD, was granted a tack of Glassichcamonich of Craggy, for nineteen years in 1841. [NRS.GD176.1453], Trinloist, Cultie, Toumvolt, and Murnich, decreets of removal in 1801. [NRS.GD23.10.643]

MCINTOSH, EDWARD, born in Inverness, emigrated to Monterey, California, around 1820, a rancher at Bodega Bay. [SHR.52.142]

MCINTOSH, FINLAY, a tenant in Glenelg, with Anne, Anne [born 1797], Donald [born 1799], emigrated via Fort William aboard the Sarah of Liverpool bound for Pictou, Nova Scotia, in June 1801. [NRS.RH2.4.87]

MCINTOSH, FINLAY, a farmer from Urquhart, with Ann, Elizabeth, Isobel, James [born 1787], Christian [born 1793], William [born 1795], and an infant, emigrated via Fort William aboard the Sarah of Liverpool bound for Pictou, Nova Scotia, in June 1801. [NRS.RH2.4.87]

MCINTOSH, GEORGE, in Duthil, an Ensign of the 42nd Regiment, was accused of murder but found not guilty in 1818. [NRS.JC11.58]

MCINTOSH, HUGH, servant of Hugh Edie, tenant in Blackhill of Kilravock, was accused of rioting at Croy Church in 1823. [NRS.AD14.23.235]

MCINTOSH, ISABELLA, in Bridgend of Corrybrough, a letter to Provost James Grant of Inverness concerning her brother-in-law John McBean, a house carpenter from Inverness in 1832. [NRS.GD23.6.679]

MCINTOSH, JAMES, born 1754 in Strathdearn, son of William Roy McIntosh of Dell and his wife Marjory McIntosh, a merchant in New York, died there on 4 November 1811. [ANY.I.176]

MCINTOSH, JAMES, and Catherine McIntosh, from Kerrowdoun, emigrated via Fort William aboard the Friends of Saltcoats master John How to Montreal in July 1802. [GkAd.59]

MCINTOSH, JAMES, born 1805 in Croy, emigrated to New York on the George of New York on 12 August 1807. [TNA.PC1.3790]

MCINTOSH, JAMES, an innkeeper in Castle Street, Inverness, was found guilty of assault and sentenced to six months in Inverness Tolbooth in 1821. [NRS.JC26.1821.112]

MACKINTOSH, JAMES, of Daviot, versus Donald MacPhail and his mother Isabell MacPhail, tenants of the Mains of Dalcross in 1828. [NRS.GD176.997]

MACKINTOSH, JAMES, of Daviot, deceased, with estate at Sandwich, Western District of Canada, letters of administration granted to his nephew Alexander Mackintosh of Mackintosh in 1835. [NRS.GD176.2060]

MCINTOSH, JAMES, a gamekeeper at Culloden, dead by 1843, uncle of John McIntosh a wright in Canada. [NRS.S/H]

MCINTOSH, JAMES, was granted a tack of Tullochclury, Moy, for twelve years in 1849. [NRS.GD176.1453]

MCINTOSH, JOHN, a farmer from Kilmorack, with Janet, Flora [born 1796], John, [born 1798], and an infant, emigrated via Fort William aboard the Sarah of Liverpool bound for Pictou, Nova Scotia, in June 1801. [NRS.RH2.4.87]

MACKINTOSH, JOHN, a messenger at arms in Fort William, a petition in 1811. [NRS.CC2.12.3.7]

MCINTOSH, JOHN, born 1735, a tailor burgess of Inverness, died on 10 November 1820, husband of Janet Fraser. [Chapel Yard gravestone, Inverness]

MACKINTOSH, JOHN, born 1816, a carpenter in Clachnacarry, died 15 May 1876, husband of Jane Ross, born 1813, died 25 November 1896. [Chapel Yard gravestone, Inverness]

MCINTOSH, JOHN, was granted a tack of Innoch, Moy, for nineteen years in 1836. [NRS.GD176.1453]

MCINTOSH, JOHN, a wright in Canada, nephew and heir of James McIntosh gamekeeper at Culloden, 1843. [NRS.S/H]

MACKINTOSH, JOHN, of Dempster Park, Inverness, born 1799, died 19 May 1859, husband of Mary Davidson, born 1799, died 29 January 1859. [Dores gravestone]

104

MCINTOSH, LACHLAN, from Inverness, a hairdresser in Hamilton, Canada West, died 11 August 1854, testament, 1854. [NRS.SC70.1.85]

MACKINTOSH, Captain LACHLAN, of Balnaspec, testament, 26 February 1800, Comm. Inverness. [NRS]

MCINTOSH, Captain LAUCHLAN, in Ballidbeg, Kingussie, a victim of theft in 1836. [NRS.AD14.36.9]

MACKINTOSH, MARGARET, born 23 December 1768 in Inverness-shire, wife of Daniel Mackintosh, died 7 November 1832 in Charleston, South Carolina. [Old Third Presbyterian gravestone, Charleston, S.C.]

MACINTOSH, MARGARET, daughter of ......MacIntosh of Dalmigavie, married Robert McBean from Tortula, British West Indies, in Inverness on 13 December 1794. [SM.56.801]

MACINTOSH, MARY, born 1767, a spinster from Baluinch, Daviot, [Deimhidh], emigrated to New York on the George of New York on 12 August 1807. [TNA.PC1.3790]

MACINTOSH, NIEL, tenant on Canna, 1818. [C.220]

MACINTOSH, PHINEAS, born 1784, second son of Alexander MacIntosh and his wife Janet McLean, died in Demerara on 4 December 1805. [Greyfriars gravestone, Inverness]

MCINTOSH, ROBERT, a farmer from Urquhart, with Janet, and Janet [born 1798], emigrated via Fort William aboard the Sarah of Liverpool bound for Pictou, Nova Scotia, in June 1801. [NRS.RH2.4.87]

MCINTOSH, ROBERT, from Glen Urquhart, settled at Sunny Brae, Nova Scotia, in 1801. [TGS.53.457]

MACKINTOSH, SIMON FRASER, born 1794, son of Campbell Mackintosh the Town Clerk of Inverness, died on 29 May 1816. [Chapel Yard gravestone, Inverness]

MCINTOSH, SWEEN, smith in Cantry, Croy, was accused of rioting at Croy Church in 1823. [NRS.AD14.23.136]

MCINTOSH, THOMAS, was granted a tack of Westertown of Duntelchaig, for fifteen years in 1837. [NRS.GD176.1453]

MACKINTOSH, WILLIAM, a travelling chapman, found guilty of stabbing in Fort William, sentenced in Inverness in September 1809 to be transported for life. [Inverness Journal.22.9.1809]

MACKINTOSH, WILLIAM, born 1798 in Inverness-shire, son of Daniel and Margaret Mackintosh, died in Charleston, South Carolina, on 25 August 1825. [Old Third Presbyterian gravestone, Charleston]

MCINTOSH, WILLIAM, a labourer in Balune of Wester Leys, Croy, was accused of rioting at Croy Church in 1823. [NRS.AD14.23.136]

MCINTOSH, WILLIAM, son of Alexander McIntosh, [1769-1802], a merchant in Inverness, settled in Surinam before 1843. [Kilmallie gravestone]

MCINTOSH, WILLIAM, was granted a tack of Eastertown of Duntelchaig, for nineteen years in 1834. [NRS.GD176.1453]

MCINTYRE, ALLAN, born in Kilmonivaig, son of Duncan McIntyre a farmer, was educated at Glasgow University, a minister in New South Wales from 1854 to 1870, died in Sydney, Australia, on 28 May 1870. [F.7.593]

MCINTYRE, ARCHIBALD WRIGHT, a merchant in Fort William, a trial in 1837. [NRS.JC11.84]; petition for sequestration in 1840. [NRS.CS279.1771]

MCINTYRE, ARCHIBALD CAMPBELL, born in 1843 in Clunes, Lochaber, died in Michigan in 1872. [S.9124]

MCINTYRE, DUNCAN, jr., a merchant in Fort William, versus John McLean and Ann McLean at Cuilcheanna, children of the deceased Helen McLean, widow of Captain Colin McLean in 1801. [NRS.CC2.2.103.2]

MACINTYRE, ISABELLA, born 17 June 1837, daughter of Reverend John MacIntyre and his wife Eliza Clark, married Duncan MacIntyre in Glenoe, Tasmania, in 1859, died on 11 September 1919. [F.4.137]

MCINTYRE, JAMES, a seaman in Kilmonivaig, was accused of assault in 1827. [NRS.AD14.27.219]

MCINTYRE, JAMES, in Pressmuckerach, Badenoch, Laggan, a victim of theft in 1829. [NRS.JC26,1829.3]

MCINTYRE, JOHN, from Inverness, graduated MA from King's College, Aberdeen, on 31 March 1809, later minister in Glen Livet. [KCA]

MCINTYRE, JOHN, from Inverness, graduated MA from King's College, Aberdeen, on 31 March 1815, later minister in Glen Shiel. [KCA]

MCINTYRE, JOHN, schoolmaster in Kilmonivaig, a petition in 1815. [NRS.GD176.1907]

MCINTYRE, JOHN, minister of Kilmonivaig, a letter, 1831. [NRS.GD170.2582]

MCINTYRE, PETER, from Inverness, graduated MA from King's College, Aberdeen, on 28 March 1799. [KCA]

MCISAAC, ALLAN, emigrated from Canna to Nova Scotia in 1812, settled at Broad Cove, Inverness County, N.S., with three sons, John, Alexander, and Donald. [C.222]

MCISAAC, ANN, from Eileen Shona, Moidart, emigrated via Driumindarroch, on the Lucy bound for Prince Edward Island in July 1790. [SCA]

MCISAAC, ARCHIBALD, a tenant on Canna in 1851. [C.299]

MACISAAC, JOHN, tenant on Canna, 1818. [C.220]

MACISAAC, JOHN, tenant on Keill, Canna, 1848. [C.297]

MACISAAC, LACHLAN, tenant on Canna, 1818. [C.220]

MACISAAC, PEGGY, a tenant on Canna in 1851. [C.299]

MACISAACH, ANGUS, a labourer in Arisaig, Catherine MacIsaach a spinner, in Arisaig, emigrated via Fort William on board the Dove of Aberdeen bound for Pictou, Nova Scotia, in 1801. [NRS.RH2.4.87.75-5]

MACISAACH, DUNCAN, a labourer in Arisaig, Mary MacIsaach a spinner, emigrated via Fort William on board the Dove of Aberdeen bound for Pictou, Nova Scotia, in 1801. [NRS.RH2.4.87.75-5]

MACISAACH, JOHN, a labourer in Arisaig, with his wife a spinner, emigrated via Fort William on board the Dove of Aberdeen bound for Pictou, Nova Scotia, in 1801. [NRS.RH2.4.87.75-5]

MCIVER, ALEXANDER, from Inverness, graduated from King's College, Aberdeen, on 30 March 1816, later schoolmaster in Glenelg, and minister on Sleat and in Dornoch. [KCA]; minister at Glenmoriston from 1824 until 1826. [F.6.453]

MACIVER, DONALD, born 1 November 1778, son of Reverend Murdoch MacIver and his wife Mary MacKenzie in Lochalsh, [Loch Aillse], a merchant in New York, died in Bermuda. [F.7.155]

MCIVER, DOROTHY, born October 1802 on Skye, [Sgitheanach], died in North Carolina on 13 August 1857. [Union gravestone, Moore County.]

MACIVER, FARQUHAR, a missionary at Glengarry in 1827, minister at Glenmoriston from 1828 until 1840, a minister in Glenshiel, died 20 September 1863, uncle of Colin Campbell a master mariner in New York. [NRS.S/H] [F.6.453]

MCIVER, JOHN, from Inverness, graduated MA from King's College, Aberdeen, on 29 March 1805, joined the British Army. [KCA]

MCIVER, MARY, born October 1802 on Skye, died in North Carolina on 1 December 18576 [Union gravestone, Moore County.]

MCKAY, ALEXANDER, with three children, from Shanvall, emigrated via Fort William aboard the Friends of Saltcoats master John How to Montreal in July 1802. [GkAd.59]

MACKAY, ALEXANDER, a cattle dealer in Tornick, Beauly, versus William Grant the tacksman of Wellhouse, 1815. [NRS.CS42.13.64]

MACKAY, Major ALEXANDER, a grazier, cattle dealer, and fish curer in Laggan, 1836. [NRS.CS97.98.M22]

MACKAY, ALEXANDER, born 1836, a letter carrier in Inverness, died 1893, husband of Margaret Bisset, born 1839, died 1892. [Old High gravestone, Inverness]

MACKAY, ALEXANDER, born 1841, son of George Mackay, died in Panama on 14 August 1888. [Chapel Yard gravestone, Inverness]

MACKAY, COLIN, born 1772 in Beauly, died in Pictou, Nova Scotia, in 1850. [Loyalist gravestone, St John, New Brunswick]

MCKAY, DONALD, born 1814, a merchant in Inverness, died 20 August 1849, husband of Isabella McPherson. [Chapel Yard gravestone, Inverness]

MACKAY, ELIZABETH, servant to Hugh Rose in Little Dalcross, was accused of rioting at Croy Church in 1823. [NRS.AD14.23.136]

MACKAY, Major JAMES, brother of Robert Mackay of Hedgefield, Inverness, emigrated to Canada before 1785, a judge in St Louis by 1817. [BM]

MCKAY, JAMES, from Inverness, graduated MA from King's College, Aberdeen, in March 1840, later an Episcopal minister in Inverness, India, and Paris. [KCA]

MACKAY, JESSIE, eldest daughter of Captain Mackay of Skail, married Roderick Young from Demerara, in Inverness on 20 June 1810. [SM.73.553], parents of a son born in Skerray, [Sgeirea], on 3 May 1812. [SM.73.558]

MCKAY, JOHN, tenant of Ardnafouran, Arisaig, emigrated via Arisaig aboard the British Queen bound for Quebec on 16 August 1790. [PAC.RG4A1, Vol.48.PP15874-5]

MACKAY, JOHN, born 1775, a vintner in Inverness, died in December 1813, husband of Mary McLean, born 1765, died 5 March 1861. [Chapel Yard gravestone, Inverness]

MACKAY, JOHN, born 1843, died 31 January 1879 at Washington Heights, Chicago, Illinois. [Drumnadrochit gravestone]

MACKAY, MARIANNE CAMERON, fourth daughter of Robert Mackay n Fort William, married Thomas Powditch of Caldera, in Valparaiso, Chile, on 29 April 1854. [EEC.22604]

MCKAY, NEIL, born 1800 in Inverness-shire, died in 1869, husband of Margaret ...., born 1801, died 1858, both from Inverness-shire. [Little Narrows gravestone, Victoria County, NS]

MCKAY, WILLIAM, from Kilmorack, with wife Janet, [1736-1814], emigrated on the Hector to Pictou, Nova Scotia, in 1773, died aged ninety-six. [Iron Bridge gravestone, New Glasgow, N.S.]

MCKAY, WILLIAM, from Inverness, graduated MA from King's College, Aberdeen, in March 1845, later minister at Killearnan. [KCA]

MACKENZIE, ALEXANDER, of Woodside, born 1764, a banker in and Commissary of Inverness, died 21 October 1838, husband of Barbara Gillanders, born 1784, died 2 September 1809. [Chapel Yard gravestone, Inverness]

MCKENZIE, ALEXANDER, born 1794 in Inverness, emigrated to Canada, an employee of the North West Company from 1813 until 1821, then in the service of the Hudson Bay Company from 1821 until he was killed by Indians in 1828. [HBRS]

MCKENZIE, ALEXANDER, and William McKenzie, in Beauly, sequestration in 1802. [NRS.CS236.M13.8]

MCKENZIE, ALEXANDER, master of the Beaufort Castle of Inverness trading with Easdale, and with Limerick, Ireland, in 1812. [NRS.E504.17.8]

MCKENZIE, ALEXANDER, son of Murdo McKenzie a chaise driver in Inverness, an apprentice shoemaker, was accused of stabbing, sentenced to one month in prison in 1811. [NRS.JC11.51]

MCKENZIE, ALEXANDER, in Ballagan, Culdoich, Croy, was accused of rioting at Croy Church in 1823. [NRS.AD14.23.235]

MCKENZIE, ALEXANDER, a merchant in Beauly in 1827. [NRS.CS233, SEQN.M2.79]

MCKENZIE, ALEXANDER, a writer in Inverness, 1830. [NRS.CS271.251]

MCKENZIE, ALEXANDER, from Inverness, graduated MA from King's College, Aberdeen, in March 1837, a Free Church minister in Nairn and in Edinburgh. [KCA]

MACKENZIE, ALEXANDER, of the Hudson Bay Company, brother and heir of Daniel MacKenzie in Inverness, 1840. [NRS.S/H]

MCKENZIE, ALEXANDER, a deer forester in Deanie, died 22 September 1851, father of John McKenzie in St John, Canada East. [NRS.S/H]

MCKENZIE, ALEXANDER, born 1820, a miller at Kingsmills, died on 11 December 1885, husband of Mary Jack, born 1824, died 28 March 1904. [Old High gravestone, Inverness]

MCKENZIE, CATHERINE, a thief, who was sentenced in Inverness on 12 September 1789 to be transported to the colonies for fourteen years. [AJ.2176]

MCKENZIE, CHARLES, born 1836, son of Charles McKenzie, died at sea in 1859. [Chapel Yard gravestone, Inverness]

MCKENZIE, Mrs CHRISTINA, from St Kilda, wife of John McKenzie, died in Cross Creek, Cumberland County, North Carolina, on 24 September 1848. [Cross Creek gravestone]

MACKENZIE, COLQUHOUN, born 1786, son of Alexander MacKenzie [1739-1825], tenant farmer in East Duthill, Deuthulph, Carrbridge, [Drochaid Charr], and his wife Anne MacQueen, [1758-1845], died in Quebec on 30 August 1828. [Carrbridge gravestone]

MCKENZIE, DANIEL, in Inverness, dead by 1840, brother of Alexander Mackenzie of the Hudson Bay Company. [NRS.S/H]

MCKENZIE, DONALD, a labourer from Kilmorack, with Ann, and John, [born 1797], emigrated via Fort William aboard the Sarah of Liverpool bound for Pictou, Nova Scotia, in June 1801. [NRS.RH2.4.87]

MCKENZIE, DONALD, a farmer from Kiltarlity, emigrated via Fort William aboard the <u>Sarah of Liverpool</u> bound for Pictou, Nova Scotia, in June 1801. [NRS.RH2.4.87]

MCKENZIE, DONALD, born 1749 in Brackachy, Inverness-shire, settled in Nova Scotia in 1812, died 22 April 1836, husband of Mary, born 1757, died 1834. [Mackenzie gravestone, Lovat, Pictou, NS]

MCKENZIE, DONALD, emigrated from Inverness to America in 1804. [Records in Rochester University, New York]

MCKENZIE, DONALD, born 1778, former British Consul in Maine, died in Inverness on 29 December 1845. [AJ.5116]

MCKENZIE, DUNCAN, master of the <u>Kelly and Lucy of Fort William</u> trading between Ballachulish and Inverness in 1820. [NRS.E504.17.8]

MCKENZIE, FARQUHAR, a labourer from Strathglass, emigrated via Fort William aboard the <u>Sarah of Liverpool</u> bound for Pictou, Nova Scotia, in June 1801. [NRS.RH2.4.87]

MCKENZIE, HECTOR, born 1808, died 12 March 1888, husband of Annie Ferguson, born 1810, died 21 January 1878, both born in Inverness-shire. [Millbrook gravestone, Pictou, NS]

MCKENZIE, HUGH, from Inverness, graduated MA from King's College, Aberdeen, later minister of the Gaelic Church in Aberdeen, joined the Free Church. [KCA]

MCKENZIE, JAMES, a baker in Petty Street, Inverness, was accused of forgery in 1831. [NRS.AD14.31.86]

MCKENZIE, JAMES, a spirit dealer in Beauly, 1846. [NRS.CS280.32.56]

MCKENZIE, JOHN, born 1745 in Inverness, emigrated to Canada around 1787, died at Green Harbour, Nova Scotia, on 10 February 1837. [Acadian Recorder, 18.3.1837]

MCKENZIE, JOHN, born 1777, a farmer from Baluich, Daviot, emigrated to New York aboard the George of New York on 12 August 1807. [TNA.PC1.3790]

MCKENZIE, JOHN, born 1804, a student in the school at Culdoich, Croy, was accused of rioting at Croy Church in 1823. [NRS.AD14.23.235]

MCKENZIE, JOHN, from Inverness, [1], graduated MA from King's College, Aberdeen, on 26 April 1813. [KCA]

MCKENZIE, JOHN, from Inverness, [2], graduated MA from King's College, Aberdeen, on 26 April 1813, a minister in Williamston, Canada. [KCA]

MCKENZIE, JOHN R., from Inverness, graduated MA from King's College, Aberdeen, in March 1829, later a Presbyterian minister in Birmingham, England. [KCA]

MCKENZIE, JOHN C., from Inverness, graduated MA from King's College, Aberdeen, in March 183. [KCA]

MCKENZIE, JOHN, the elder, a merchant and shipowner in Stornaway, trading with Memel [Klaipeda] and Archangel, a letter-book between 1795 and 1836. [NRS.CS96.4475]

MACKENZIE, Dr JOHN, born 1787, in Grant's Close, Inverness, died 18 December 1865, husband of Margaret Munro, born 1813, died 16 January 1875. [Chapel Yard gravestone, Inverness]

MCKENZIE, JOHN, born 1793 in Inverness-shire, a cabinet maker in Charleston, South Carolina, was naturalised there on 6 August 1847. [NARA.M1183.1]

MCKENZIE, JOHN, minister at Glenmoriston from 1818 until 1823. [F.6.453]

MCKENZIE, JOHN, in St John, Canada East, son and heir of Alexander McKenzie a deer forester in Deanie, who died on 22 September 1851, [NRS.S/H]

MCKENZIE, KENNETH, born 1761, a blacksmith in Inverness, died in June 1823, husband of Margaret........., parents of John McKenzie, born 1792, a blacksmith in Inverness, died on 19 September 1867. [Old High gravestone, Inverness]

MCKENZIE, KENNETH, son of Simon McKenzie in 13 Castle Wynd, Inverness, was accused of housebreaking and theft in Castle Street, Inverness, in 1830. [NRS.AD14.30.81]

MCKENZIE, MARGARET, born 1814 in Ardersier, wife of Alexander Ross, died in Oakville, Upper Canada, on 30 March 1841. [AJ.4875]

MCKENZIE, MARGARET, born 1782 in Inverness, a servant now a widow and pauper in Essich in 1857, mother of William, born 1809, a tailor in Canada. [IPR]

MCKENZIE, MURDOCH, a midwife in Garlin of Abernethy, accused of homicide in 1812. [NRS.AD14.12.80]

MCKENZIE, RODERICK, born 1778 in Inverness-shire, died at Mount Pleasant, West River, Nova Scotia, on 21 April 1868, emigrated to NS in 1801, husband of Ann, born 1786, died 1867. [MacKenzie cemetery, Lovat, Pictou, NS]

MCKENZIE, SIMON, son of William McKenzie, [1748-1838] schoolmaster at Leys, and his wife Janet Chisholm, [1754-1815], settled in Caledonia, Livingstone County, New York. [Dunlichty gravestone]

MCKENZIE, THOMAS H., settled in Dundas, Canada West, before 1855. [Kirkton of Ardesier gravestone]

MCKENZIE, WILLIAM, a farmer from Urquhart, with Flory, Isobel [born 1796], and John [born 1799], emigrated via Fort William aboard the Sarah of Liverpool bound for Pictou, Nova Scotia, in June 1801. [NRS.RH2.4.87]

MCKENZIE, WILLIAM, born 1748, schoolmaster at Leys, died 1838, husband of Janet Chisholm, born 1754, died 1815, parents of Donald McKenzie and Simon McKenzie, who settled in Caledonia, Livingstone County, New York. [Dunlichty gravestone]

MCKENZIE, WILLIAM, a labourer from Strathglass, with Catherine, emigrated via Fort William aboard the Sarah of Liverpool bound for Pictou, Nova Scotia, in June 1801. [NRS.RH2.4.87]

MCKENZIE, WILLIAM, master of the Tay of Fort William trading between Easdale and Inverness in 1817. [NRS.E504.17.8]

MCKINZIE, ALEXANDER, from Urquhart, emigrated via Fort William aboard the Friends of Saltcoats master John How to Montreal in July 1802. [GkAd.59]

MACKICHAN, DUGALD, born 1801 son of Finlay MacKichan a merchant in Ardchattan, was educated at the University of Glasgow, minister at Barney's River, Pictou, Nova Scotia, then minister at Daviot and Dunlichty from 1845 until his death on 5 December 1858. [F.6.449]; husband of Isabella MacPhie, born in Appin on 15 June 1807, died at the Manse of Lochgilphead on 24 March 1867. [Daviot gravestone]

MCKILLICAN, JOHN, born 1744 in Croy, graduated MA from King's College, Aberdeen, in 1764, a missionary at Boleskine and later at Fort William, minister at Dores from 1785until his death on 13 June 1819. [F.6.451]

MCKINNON, ALEXANDER, his wife and three children, emigrated via Fort William aboard the Friends of Saltcoats master John How to Montreal in July 1802. [GkAd.59]

116

MCKINNON, ALEXANDER, from Inverness, graduated MA from King's College, Aberdeen, on 30 March 1807. [KCA]

MACKINNON, ALLAN, a tenant on Canna in 1851. [C.299]

MACKINNON, ANGUS, a tenant on Sanday, Canna, in 1848, 1851. [C.297/299]

MACKINNON, ARCHIBALD, [1], a tenant on Canna in 1851. [C.299]

MACKINNON, ARCHIBALD, [2], a tenant on Canna in 1851. [C.299]

MACKINNON, CHARLES, a tenant in Tarbert, Canna, in 1848, 1851. [C.297/299]

MCKINNON, DONALD, from Inverness, graduated MA from King's College, Aberdeen, on 2 April 1804, later minister in Sleat and Strath . [KCA]

MCKINNON, DONALD, his wife and six children, from Donie, emigrated via Fort William aboard the Friends of Saltcoats master John How to Montreal in July 1802. [GkAd.59]

MCKINNON, DONALD, from North Uist, settled in North Carolina, admin. 1803, PCC. [TNA]

MCKINNON, DONALD DOW, a grasskeeper in Kilmally, Inverness, guilty of sheep stealing, was sentenced to transportation for fourteen years in 1806. [NRS.JC11.48]

MCKINNON, DONALD, in Strath, Skye, a victim of assault in the Caledonian Hotel, Dingwall, in 1837. [NRS.AD14.37.36; JC26.1837.108]

MACKINNON, DONALD, a tenant in Tarbert, Canna, in 1848. [C.297]

MCKINNON, DONALD, born 1817, a farmer in Urchany, Beauly, died in America on 20 June 1888. [Beauly Priory gravestone]

MCKINNON, DUNCAN, from Caum, emigrated via Fort William aboard the <u>Friends of Saltcoats</u> master John How to Montreal in July 1802. [GkAd.59]

MACKINNON, HECTOR's widow, a tenant on Canna in 1851. [C.299]

MACKINNON, HUGH, a tenant on Canna in 1851. [C.299]

MCKINNON, JOHN, from Inverness, graduated MA from King's College, Aberdeen, on 2 April 1804. [KCA]

MCKINNON, JOHN, born 1768 on Skye, died in Savannah, Georgia, on 5 November 1825. [Augusta Herald, 17.7.1821]

MACKINNON, JOHN, a tenant on Keill, Canna in 1848, 1851. [C.297/299]

MACKINNON, JOHN, a tenant in Sanday, Canna, 1848. [C.297]

MACKINNON, LACHLAN, a tenant on Sanday, Canna in 1848, 1851. [C.297/299]

MACKINNON, NEIL's widow, tenant on Canna, 1818. [C.220]

MACKINNON, ..., a widow, a tenant in Keill, Canna in 1848, 1851. [C.297/299]

MCLACHLAN, DUGALD, a shipowner, grazier and wool dealer in Cornanan, Fort William, sequestration, 1824. [NRS.CS233.M2.7.1]

MCLACHLAN, EWEN, from Inverness, graduated MA from King's College, Aberdeen, on 27 March 1800, later Rector of Aberdeen Grammar School. [KCA]

MCLACHLAN, LEWIS, in Fasfern, [Am Fasadh Fearna], Fort William, applied to settle in Canada on 25 January 1819. [TNA.CO384.5.19]

MCLACHLAN, WILLIAM, born 1749, a farmer in Balmavoich, Dores, [Dubhras], with his wife Margaret Fraser born 1756, and children Catherine born 1779, Alexander born 1787, Andrew born 1790, Donald born 1795, Lachlan born 1797, Isabel born 1799, and James born 1803, emigrated to New York on board the George of New York on 12 August 1807. [TNA.PC1.3790]

MCLAUCHLAN, ALEXANDER FRASER, eldest son of Reverend James McLauchlan in Moy, assistant surgeon on the Madras Establishment, died in Nagpure, India, on 23 June 1825. [SM.97.127]

MCLAUCHLAN, Reverend JAMES, minister at Moy, a letter, 1823. [NRS.GD136.553]

MCLAUGHLAN, DUGALD, in Jamaica, later in Calait, Inverness, testament, 4 July 1800, Comm. Argyll. [NRS]

MCLEAN, ALEXANDER, a farmer from Moidart, Marion a spinner, a son born 1798, and an infant, emigrated via Fort William on board the Dove of Aberdeen bound for Pictou, Nova Scotia, in 1801. [NRS.RH2.4.87.75-5]

MCLEAN, ALEXANDER, a tenant in Urquhart, with Margaret, Becky [born 1797], and Ann [born 1799], emigrated via Fort William aboard the Sarah of Liverpool bound for Pictou, Nova Scotia, in June 1801. [NRS.RH2.4.87]

MCLEAN, ALEXANDER, from Inverness, graduated MA from King's College, Aberdeen, on 30 March 1801. [KCA]

MCLEAN, ALEXANDER, in Petty Street, Inverness, was accused of housebreaking and theft in Castle Street, Inverness, in 1830. [NRS.AD14.30.81]

MCLEAN, ALEXANDER, and his wife Catherine McVarish, from Inverness-shire, parents of Isabella McLean, born 1810, died 1865. [St Andrew's gravestone, Judique, Cape Breton]

MCLEAN, ALLAN, a labourer in Alvie, accused of non payment of duty on malt whisky, in 1829. [NRS.CE21.8]

MCLEAN, ANGUS, Duncan McLean, Janet McLean, and one child, from Munerigy, emigrated via Fort William aboard the Friends of Saltcoats master John How to Montreal in July 1802. [GkAd.59]

MCLEAN, CATHARINE, from Caum, emigrated via Fort William aboard the Friends of Saltcoats master John How to Montreal in July 1802. [GkAd.59]

MCLEAN, CHARLES, born 29 January 1846 in Kiltearn, son of Reverend Alexander McLean and his wife Margaret Davidson, settled in British Columbia. [F.7.44]

MCLEAN, CHRISTY, from Invergarry, emigrated via Fort William aboard the Friends of Saltcoats master John How to Montreal in July 1802. [GkAd.59]

MACLEAN, DONALD, tenant on Canna, 1818. [C.220]

MCLEAN, DONALD, born 1799 in Glen Elg, died 4 December 1898, husband of Mary Symonds, born 1804, died 1871. [McLean cemetery, Boulardie Island, Cape Breton, N.S.]

MCLEAN, DONALD, [1836-1908], and his wife Jessie MacMillan, [1846-1908], parents of Alexander McLean, born 1874, died in Nelson, British Columbia, on 13 August 1913. [Old Kilmore gravestone, Drumnadrochit]

MCLEAN, DUNCAN, and wife, from Caum, emigrated via Fort William aboard the Friends of Saltcoats master John How to Montreal in July 1802. [GkAd.59]

MCLEAN, DUNCAN, and his wife, from Munerigy, emigrated via Fort William aboard the Friends of Saltcoats master John How to Montreal in July 1802. [GkAd.59]

MCLEAN, EWAN, his wife, Donald McLean, Catherine McLean, Mary McLean, and four children, from Aberchalder, emigrated via Fort William aboard the Friends of Saltcoats master John How to Montreal in July 1802. [GkAd.59]

MCLEAN, ISABELLA, born 1810, daughter of Alexander and Catherine McVarish in Inverness-shire, died 9 April 1865. [Judique gravestone, Inverness County, NS]

MCLEAN, JOHN, son of Nigel McLean a schoolmaster in Urquhart, a student in Marischal College, Aberdeen, in 1846. [MCA]

MCLEAN, JOHN, in Knockbain, born 1740, died 26 February 1830, husband of Ann Fraser, born 1756, parents of John McLean, born 1802, after 21 years in Demerara, died in Wardlaw on 28 May 1851. [Wardlaw gravestone]

MACLEAN, JOHN, tenant on Keill, Canna, 1848. [C.297]

MCLEAN, JOHN HUGH, died 1858, and his wife Catherine Thomson, died 1888, parents of William McLean, born 1855, minister of the Presbyterian church in Cogswell, Sargent County, North Dakota, died 3 August 1904. [Croy gravestone]

MCLEAN, MARY, with Katherine McLean, from Laddy, emigrated via Fort William aboard the Friends of Saltcoats master John How, bound to Montreal in July 1802. [GkAd.59]

MCLEAN, MARGARET, born 1812, wife of James Fraser a gardener in Inverness, died on 17 February 1869. [Old High gravestone, Inverness]

MACLEAN, MARJORY, born 1763, daughter of Charles MacLean of Dochgarroch, and widow of Alexander Lee a merchant, died in Inverness on 29 May 1820. [SM.86.190]

MCLEAN, NIEL, from Inverness, graduated MA from King's College, Aberdeen, on 30 March 1801, later a minister of Tyree and the Small Isles . [KCA]

MCLEAN, RODERICK, born 1845, died in America in 1896. [Kilmorack gravestone]

MCLEAN, Mrs S., born 1797, from Inverness, died in Buenos Ayres, Argentina, in 1871. ['Scots on the River Plate', 365]

MCLEAN, WILLIAM, a labourer from Beaulyside, with Janet, emigrated via Fort William aboard the Sarah of Liverpool bound for Pictou, Nova Scotia, in June 1801. [NRS.RH2.4.87]

MCLELLAN, ARCHIBALD, a farmer from Brincory of Morar, with Isobel, Angus [born 1799], and Mary [born 1798], emigrated via Fort William aboard the Sarah of Liverpool bound for Pictou, Nova Scotia, in June 1801. [NRS.RH2.4.87]

MACLELLAN, ARCHIBALD, a farmer in Bracora, Morar, Isobel MacLellan emigrated via Fort William aboard the Friends of Saltcoats master John How to Montreal in July 1802. [GkAd.59]

MCLELLAND, ARCHIBALD, a house carpenter in Glen Elg, accused of forgery, guilty, sentenced to transportation for fourteen years in 1807. [NRS.JC26.1807.41]

MCLELLAN, ARCHIBALD, born 1798, tenant in Kyles Morar, Glen Elg, was accused of the murder of his wife Catherine on the seashore at Glen Nevis in 1830. [NRS.AD14.30.76]

MACLELLAN, ..., a spinner, with Angus born 1799, and Mary born 1798 emigrated via Fort William on board the Sarah of Liverpool bound for Pictou, Nova Scotia, in 1801. [NRS.RH2.4.87/66-71]

MACLELLAN, DONALD, tenant in Morar, Mary a spinner, Karin born 1794, Margaret born 1796, Patrick born 1798, and Alexander born 1799, emigrated via Fort William on board the Dove of Aberdeen bound for Pictou, Nova Scotia, in 1801. [NRS.RH2.4.87.75-5]

MCLELLAN, DONALD, born 1804 in Morar, died 26 January 1890 on Cape Breton, his wife Mary McPherson, born 1819, died 3 February 1894. [Broad Cove gravestone, Cape Breton]

MCLELLAN, DONALD, a labourer at Kirkton of Glen Elg, accused of assault, found not guilty in 1815. [NRS.JC26.1815.60]

MCLENNAN, JOHN, a labourer from Aird, with Christian, and Kate [born 1798], emigrated via Fort William aboard the Sarah of Liverpool bound for Pictou, Nova Scotia, in June 1801. [NRS.RH2.4.87]

MCLENNAN, HUGH, born 1776 in Inverness, died in Halifax, Nova Scotia, on 23 December 1820. [Acadian Recorder, 23.12.1820]

MCLENNAN, JOHN FERGUSON, from Inverness, graduated MA from King's College, Aberdeen, in March 1849. [KCA]

MCLENNAN, JOHN, born 1850 in Inverness-shire, died 20 January 1881. [St George gravestone, Port Elizabeth, South Africa]

MCLENNAN, KENNETH, son of John McLennan a pensioner in Castle Street, Inverness, was accused of housebreaking and theft there in 1830. [NRS.AD14.30.81]

MCLENNAN, KENNETH, born 1817, died 2 August 1867 in Inverness, husband of Ann ......, born 1829, died 10 March 1881. [Old High gravestone, Inverness]

MCLENNAN, KENNETH, born 1783, a sawyer in Drumchardy, died 11 June 1852, husband of Janet Sutherland, born 1782, died 25 February 1874. [Wardlaw gravestone]

123

MCLENNAN, MURDO, a farmer from Aird, with Janet, Murdo [born 1798], emigrated via Fort William aboard the <u>Sarah of Liverpool</u> bound for Pictou, Nova Scotia, in June 1801. [NRS.RH2.4.87]

MCLEOD, AENEAS, from Inverness, graduated MA from King's College, Aberdeen, in March 1839. [KCA]

MCLEOD, ALEXANDER, died in Dominica in 179-, possibly from Kirkhill, Inverness, testament, 1798, Comm. Edinburgh. [NRS]

MCLEOD, ALEXANDER, of Balmeanach, sometime Captain of the 78th Regiment of Foot, testament, 27 August 1799, Comm. Inverness. [NRS]

MACLEOD, ALEXANDER, with John MacArthur, tenants on Canna, 1818. [C.220]

MCLEOD, ANDREW, born 1739 in Inverness-shire, died 1 March 1816 in North Carolina. [Hoke County gravestone, N.C.]

MACLEOD, ANGUS, tenant on Canna, 1818. [C.220]

MCLEOD, ANGUS, son of Donald McLeod from Inverness, emigrated to Canada in 1825, 'one of the Niagara volunteers who defeated McKenzie at Toronto'. [GSP.654]

MCLEOD, Dr DONALD, born 1754 on Skye, settled in Georgia in 1779, died in Savannah on 20 June 1802. [Colonial Museum and Savannah Advertiser, 22.6.1802]

MCLEOD, DONALD, a labourer in Galder, Glen Elg, was accused of assault, found guilty and sentenced to nine months imprisonment in 1821. [NRS.AD14.21.131; JC26.1821.112]

MCLEOD, GEORGE, son of Donald McLeod from Inverness, a schoolmaster on Amherst Island, near Kingston, Upper Canada, in 1841. [GSP.654]

MCLEOD, JOHN, from Inverness, graduated MA from King's College, Aberdeen, on 28 March 1801. [KCA]

MCLEOD, JOHN, a tenant on Canna in 1851. [C.299]

MCLEOD, KATHERINE, youngest daughter of Alexander Norman McLeod of Harris, married M. de Bourboulon, the French Minister to China, in Baltimore, Maryland, on 28 April 1851. [W.1234]

MCLEOD, KENNETH, in Kirkton of Glen Elg, was accused of assault in 1821. [NRS.AD14.21.131]

MCLEOD, LEWIS CHARLES, from Inverness, graduated MA from King's College, Aberdeen, on 31 March 1815, later an MD in the Service of the East India Company. [KCA]

MCLEOD, MARY, daughter of Duncan McLeod in Garraford, Kilmuir, Skye, guilty of child murder, was banished from Scotland for life in 1806. [NRS.JC11.48]

MCLEOD, MARY ANN, youngest daughter of Captain McLeod of Perefiler, Skye, died in Allahabad, East Indies, on 12 July 1839. [SG.818]

MACLEOD, MURDOCH, tenant on Keill, Canna, 1848. [C.297]

MCLEOD, MURDOCH, sr., a tenant on Canna in 1851. [C.299]

MCLEOD, MURDOCH, jr, a tenant on Canna in 1851. [C.299]

MCLEOD, NORMAN, in Kirkton of Glen Elg, was accused of assault, found guilty and sentenced to nine months imprisonment in 1821. [NRS.AD14.21.131; JC26.1821.112]

MCLEOD, RODERICK, from Inverness, graduated MA from King's College, Aberdeen, on 31 March 1815, later minister of Bracadale and Snizort, later joined the Free Church. [KCA]

MCLEOD, RODERICK, from Inverness, graduated MA from King's College, Aberdeen, in March 1818. [KCA]

MCLEOD, THOMAS, born 1795 in Inverness-shire, died 21 March 1868, wife Nancy born 1797, died 1868. [Pioneer cemetery, Pictou, Nova Scotia]

MCLEOD, WILLIAM, born 1790, a house carpenter in Inverness, died 25 April 1841, husband of Margaret McKenzie. [Chapel Yard gravestone, Inverness]

MCMASTER, JOHN, son of Duncan McMaster in the Kirkton of Glenelg, was accused of stealing goats in 1837. [NRS.AD14.37.18]

MCMASTER, MARY, from Glen Spean, emigrated via Fort William aboard the Friends of Saltcoats master John How to Montreal in July 1802. [GkAd.59]

MCMILLAN, ALEXANDER, his wife and one child, from Callich, emigrated via Fort William aboard the Friends of Saltcoats master John How to Montreal in July 1802. [GkAd.59]

MACMILLAN, ALEXANDER, son of John McMillan a crofter, a shepherd in Uchnachan, Kilmonivaig, was accused of theft in 1824. [NRS.AD14.24.84]

MCMILLAN, ANGUS, formerly a drover in Lochaber, later in America in 1798. [NRS.CS17.1.17/203]

MCMILLAN, ANGUS, his wife and two children, from Arkaig, emigrated via Fort William aboard the Friends of Saltcoats master John How to Montreal in July 1802. [GkAd.59]

MCMILLAN, ARCHIBALD, Mary McMillan, Katherine McMillan, Miles McMillan, from Inverskilroy, emigrated via Fort William aboard the Friends of Saltcoats master John How to Montreal in July 1802. [GkAd.59]

126

MCMILLAN, ARCHIBALD, his wife and five children, from Murlaggan, emigrated via Fort William aboard the <u>Friends of Saltcoats</u> master John How to Montreal in July 1802. [GkAd.59]

MCMILLAN, DONALD, his wife and four children, from Tomdoun, emigrated via Fort William aboard the <u>Friends of Saltcoats</u> master John How to Montreal in July 1802. [GkAd.59]

MCMILLAN, DONALD, and his wife, from Achintore, emigrated via Fort William aboard the <u>Friends of Saltcoats</u> master John How to Montreal in July 1802. [GkAd.59]

MCMILLAN, DUNCAN, his wife, John McMillan, Margaret McMillan, from Aberchalder, emigrated via Fort William aboard the <u>Friends of Saltcoats</u> master John How to Montreal in July 1802. [GkAd.59]

MCMILLAN, DOUGALD, tenant of Drumulu, Moidart, with family, emigrated via Arisaig aboard the <u>British Queen</u> bound for Quebec on 16 August 1790. [PAC.RG4A1, Vol.48.PP15874]

MCMILLAN, DUGALD, his wife and one child, from Inchlagan, emigrated via Fort William aboard the <u>Friends of Saltcoats</u> master John How to Montreal in July 1802. [GkAd.59]

MCMILLAN, DUNCAN, his wife, Catherine McMillan, Effy McMillan, and four children from Shanvall, [Seann Bhaile], emigrated via Fort William aboard the <u>Friends of Saltcoats</u> master John How to Montreal in July 1802. [GkAd.59]

MCMILLAN, EWEN, wife, and three children, from Coinich, emigrated via Fort William aboard the <u>Friends of Saltcoats</u> master John How to Montreal in July 1802. [GkAd.59]

MCMILLAN, EWAN, his wife, Mary McMillan, Peggy McMillan, Donald McMillan, Ewan McMillan, from Lubriach, emigrated via Fort William aboard the Friends of Saltcoats master John How to Montreal in July 1802. [GkAd.59]

MCMILLAN, E., his wife and four children, from Corrybuy, emigrated via Fort William aboard the Friends of Saltcoats master John How to Montreal in July 1802. [GkAd.59]

MCMILLAN, HUGH, born 29 April 1842, son of Donald McMillan, a farmer in Leys, and his wife Anne Cumming, died in Queensland, Australia, on 17 August 1878. [Kilmore gravestone, Drumnadrochit]

MACMILLAN, JOHN ROY, born 1770 in Lochaber, [Loch Abar], with Mary Grant his wife, emigrated to Canada, settled in Glengarry County, buried at St Columba's, Kirkhill, Glengarry County. [CMM]

MCMILLAN, JOHN, with his wife Catherine Campbell, in Glen Urquhart, emigrated on board the Sarah in 1801 bound for Pictou, Nova Scotia, settled in Churchville. [TGS.53.455]

MCMILLAN, JOHN, a blacksmith in Strathglass, with Catherine, Elizabeth [born 1794], and William [born 1796] emigrated via Fort William aboard the Sarah of Liverpool bound for Pictou, Nova Scotia, in June 1801. [NRS.RH2.4.87]

MCMILLAN, JOHN, his wife, Duncan McMillan, Betty McMillan, from Coinich, emigrated via Fort William aboard the Friends of Saltcoats master John How to Montreal in July 1802. [GkAd.59]

MCMILLAN, JOHN, his wife, from Shanvall, [Seann Bhaile], emigrated via Fort William aboard the Friends of Saltcoats master John How to Montreal in July 1802. [GkAd.59]

MCMILLAN, JOHN, his wife, Mary McMillan, Margaret McMillan, Catherine McMillan, from Muick, emigrated via Fort William aboard the Friends of Saltcoats master John How to Montreal in July 1802. [GkAd.59]

MCMILLAN, JOHN, with his wife and eight children, from Glen Alpine, Lochaber, emigrated to Nova Scotia on board the Norah in 1803, settled in Antigonish, N.S. [SG.3.97]

MCMILLAN, JOHN, his wife, Ewen McMillan, and five children, from Corsuck, emigrated via Fort William aboard the Friends of Saltcoats master John How to Montreal in July 1802. [GkAd.59]

MCMILLAN, JOHN, from Glen Urquhart, graduated from King's College, Aberdeen, in 1860, later a schoolmaster in South Africa. [KCA.311]

MCMILLAN, KATHERINE, Mary McMillan, Peggy McMillan, and one child, from Shanvall, emigrated via Fort William aboard the Friends of Saltcoats master John How to Montreal in July 1802. [GkAd.59]

MCMILLAN, MAIREAD, from Aberchalder, emigrated via Fort William aboard the Friends of Saltcoats master John How to Montreal in July 1802. [GkAd.59]

MCMILLAN, WILLIAM, son of Finlay McMillan, with his wife Bella McKenzie, emigrated to Nova Scotia on board the Aurora in 1801, settled in Churchville. [TGS.53.455]

MCMILLAN, WILLIAM, a labourer from Urquhart, emigrated via Fort William aboard the Sarah of Liverpool bound for Pictou, Nova Scotia, in June 1801. [NRS.RH2.4.87]

MCMILLAN, WILLIAM, from Glen Urquhart, [Gleann Urchaidain]' with his wife Penuel MacDougall, and sons Donald and Alpine, emigrated to Pictou, Nova Scotia, in 1818, settled at the South River, Antigonish, N.S. [TGS.53.448]

129

MCNAB, a widow, born 1756, residing behind Drummond Hill, Laggan, a petition, 1832. [NRS.GD112.11.9.8.7]

MCNAIR, RODERICK, born 1789 in Inverness-shire, died 22 October 1856. [Antigonish Catholic cemetery, NS]

MCNAUGHTON, DUNCAN, in Unachan, Kilmonivaig, a victim of assault in 1837. [NRS.AD14.37.1; JC26.1837.70]

MCNAUGHTON, DONALD, son of Donald McNaughton and his wife Margaret Cameron in Fort William, died in Woodside, Auckland, New Zealand, in 1860. [Inverlochy gravestone]

MCNAUGHTON, DUNCAN, son of Duncan McNaughton, died 1825, and his wife Margery Cameron, died 1828, died at Woodside, Auckland, New Zealand, in 1860. [Craigs gravestone]

MCNAUGHTON, PETER, born 1799 in Comrie, son of John McNaughton a farmer, graduated MA from Glasgow University in 1821, emigrated to Canada, returned to Scotland in 1844, minister at Dores from 1844 until 1846 when he returned to Vaughan, Canada, then to a parish in Pickering, Ontario, until 1855, died 10 May 1878. [F.6.452]

MACNEILL, DONALD, of Canna, proprietor there from 1827 until his death on 10 November 1848, father of Donald MacNeill born 1833. [C.295][NRS.GD201.2.63]

MCNEILL, ISABEL, a thief, who was sentenced in Inverness on 27 April 1789 to be transported for life. [AJ.2156]

MACNISHIE, WILLIAM, son of John MacNishie in Petty, Inverness, a student in Marischal College in 1790s. [MCA]

MCPHAIL, ANGUS, was granted a tack of Mid Lairg and Croygorstan, Strathnairn, for nineteen years in 1833. [NRS.GD176.1453]

MCPHAIL, JAMES, born 27 February 1766, son of Hector MacPhail, graduated MA from King's College, Aberdeen, in 1785, minister of Daviot and Dunlichty, from 1802 until his death on 1 July 1839, [F.6.1839]; a petition, 1812. [NRS.GD176.1743]

MCPHEE, ALEXANDER, with Alexander McPhee, Catherine McAlpin, Mary McPhee, Margaret McPhee, Anny McPhee and a child, from Aberchalder, [Obar Chaladair], emigrated via Fort William aboard the Friends of Saltcoats master John How to Montreal in July 1802. [GkAd.59]

MCPHEE, DONALD, a smith, a tenant on Canna in 1851. [C.299]

MCPHERSON, ALEXANDER, born 1818, a boot and shoemaker in Kinloss, died 5 March 1853. [Brachlich gravestone]

MCPHEE, DONALD, with his wife, and Anne Kennedy and Janet Marshall from Aberchalder, [Obar Chaladair], emigrated via Fort William aboard the Friends of Saltcoats master John How to Montreal in July 1802. [GkAd.59]

MCPHERSON, ALEXANDER, a goldsmith in Inverness from 1788 until his death in 1790. [Inverness Library]

MCPHERSON, ANDREW, born 1787 in Inverness-shire, died 28 March 1870, husband of Lucy McDiarmaid, born 1797, died 1878. [Lower Middle River gravestone, Pictou, NS]

MCPHERSON, ANGUS, born 1789, a farmer in Balnavoich, Dores, [Dubhras], emigrated to New York on the George of New York on 12 August 1807. [TNA.PC1.3790]

MCPHERSON, ANGUS NEILSON, born 12 July 1812 in Cluny, son of Angus McPherson and his wife Margaret Neilson, settled in Philadelphia as a mechanic, died in Fieldsboro, New Jersey, on 31 July 1876. [AP]

MCPHERSON, ANN, was accused of obstructing officers of the Revenue at Strone, Kingussie, in 1823. [NRS.JC26.1823.12]

MCPHERSON, CHRISTINA, eldest daughter of ..... McPherson of Culcabock, died in Queenstown, Upper Canada, on 10 January 1837. [AJ.4652]

MCPHERSON, DONALD, of Culenline, testament, 18 June 1791, Comm. Inverness, [NRS]

MCPHERSON, Lieutenant D., in Kingussie, a letter to Provost James Grant of Inverness in 1809. [NRS.GD23.6.455]

MCPHERSON, DANIEL, born 1752 in Inverness, settled in Sorel, Quebec, and in 1790 in Douglastown, Gaspe, Quebec, as a fishmonger, died in St Thomas, Montmagny, in June 1840. [The Scot in New France, Montreal 1881]

MCPHERSON, DONALD, a farmer from Strathglass, with Mary, and Ann, emigrated via Fort William aboard the Sarah of Liverpool bound for Pictou, Nova Scotia, in June 1801. [NRS.RH2.4.87]

MCPHERSON, DONALD, in Jamaica, later in Strathdearn, testament, 24 May 1803, Comm. Inverness. [NRS]

MCPHERSON, DONALD, born 1807, in Carriewring, Kingussie, was accused of theft in 1835. [NRS.AD14.35.4]

MACPHERSON, DONALD, a farmer in Balchree of Petty, then in Blarnaphat, dead by 1851. [NRS.S/H]

MCPHERSON, DONALD, was accused of obstructing officers of the Revenue at Strone, Kingussie, in 1823, sentenced to one month in prison. [NRS.JC26.1823.12]

MCPHERSON, DUNCAN, Customs Collector of Inverness in 1826. [NRS.CE7.18.1]

MCPHERSON, EMILY, in Muckcoul, Laggan, a victim of theft in 1835. [NRS.AD.14.35.4]

MCPHERSON, EWAN, born in Kingussie, died in Clarendon, Jamaica, on 3 January 1840. [AJ.4813]

MCPHERSON, EVAN, in Kingussie, a sequestration petition in 1846. [NRS.CS279.1753]

MCPHERSON, FRANCES PASIA, third daughter of McPherson of Culcabock, married John Hamilton, youngest son of Robert Hamilton of Queenston, Upper Canada, there on 7 April 1829. [S.981.351]

MCPHERSON, Captain GEORGE, of Ballvan, a Justice of the Peace, a victim of the riot at Croy Church in 1823. [NRS.AD14.23.35]

MCPHERSON, HELEN, from Culcabock, Inverness, married John MacAulay of Kingston, in Montreal, Quebec, on 22 October 1833. [AJ.4482]

MCPHERSON, HUGH, a labourer from Strathglass, emigrated via Fort William aboard the Sarah of Liverpool bound for Pictou, Nova Scotia, in June 1801. [NRS.RH2.4.87]

MCPHERSON, ISOBEL, widow of William Mackintosh of Aberarder, testament, 25 April 1796, Comm. Inverness. [NRS]

MCPHERSON, JAMES, of Killihuntly, testament, 3 March 1790, Comm. Inverness. [NRS]

MCPHERSON, JAMES, of Belville, testament, 8 April 1799, Comm. Inverness. [NRS]

MACPHERSON, JAMES, son of James MacPherson of Ardesier, graduated MA from Marischal College, Aberdeen, in 1804. [MCA]

MCPHERSON, JAMES WILLIAM, son of George in Inverness-shire, a student at Marischal College, Aberdeen, in 1830s. [MCA]

MCPHERSON, JOHN, of Inverhall, testament, 28 September 1793, [NRS]

MCPHERSON, JOHN, of Invernahawn, testament, 20 November 1800. [NRS]

MCPHERSON, JOHN, in St Thomas in the East, Surrey, Jamaica, died in August 1800, son of John McPherson of Moerhahawe, testament, 1801, Comm. Edinburgh. [NRS]

MCPHERSON, JOHN, a writer in Kingussie, trustee of Donald Clark a road contractor in Gargask, 1814-1815. [NRS.CS96.889]

MCPHERSON, JOHN, jr., in Crubinmore, Laggan, accused of theft in 1836. [NRS.AD14.36.9]

MCPHERSON, Captain LAUCHLAN, in Woolhouse, Ballidbeg, Kingussie, a victim of theft in 1836. [NRS.AD14.36.9]

MCPHERSON, ROBERT, born 1772, son of Angus McPherson and his wife Ann Grant in Rothiemurchus, died in Jamaica in 1839. [Rothiemurchus gravestone]

MCPHERSON, SOPHIA, was accused of obstructing officers of the Revenue at Strone, Kingussie, in 1823, sentenced to one month in prison. [NRS.JC26.1823.12]

MCPHERSON, WILLIAM, in Vere, Middlesex, Jamaica, died there on 25 May 1798, testament, 1820, Comm. Edinburgh. [NRS]

MACPHERSON, WILLIAM, born 1780, died 9 December 1831, husband of Ann Burgess. [Old High gravestone, Inverness]

MCQUEEN, ALEXANDER, was granted a tack of Easter Ruthven, Strathnairn, for nineteen years in 1836 [NRS.GD176.1453]

MCQUEEN, ALEXANDER, and his wife Jessie McGregor, parents of Elsie McQueen, born 1851, wife of G. W. Hope, died in Prosperine Hospital, North Queensland, Australia, on 23 December 1919. [Duthil gravestone]

MCQUEEN, DONALD, of Corrybrough, was granted a tack of Polochaig for nineteen years in 1825. [NRS.GD176.1453]

MCQUEEN, Captain DONALD, of Corrybrough, in the parish of Moy and Dalrossie, and his brother Hugh McQueen, 1826. [NRS.GD23.4.264]

MCQUEEN, ELSIE, born 1851, daughter of Alexander McQueen and his wife Jessie McGregor, wife of G. W. Hope, died in Prosperpine Hospital, North Queensland, Australia, on 23 December 1919. [Duthil gravestone,]

MCQUEEN, FINLAY, born 1794, his wife Christy born 1802, son Malcolm born 1828, daughter Rachel born 1833, and son John born 1839, from St Kilda, emigrated via Liverpool aboard the Priscilla bound for Victoria, Australia, on 15 October 1852. [NRS.HD4/5]

MCQUEEN, FINLAY, jr., born 1808, his wife Catherine born 1808, son Donald born 1834, son Neil born 1845, son Finlay born 1848, and daughter Mary born 1851, from St Kilda, emigrated via Liverpool aboard the Priscilla bound for Victoria, Australia, on 15 October 1852. [NRS.HD4/5]

MCQUEEN, WILLIAM, from Inverness, graduated MA from King's College, Aberdeen, in March 1818. [KCA]

MCQUARRIE, CHARLES, in Moy, a letter from his cousin Lachlan McQuarrie late of Ulva in 1790. [NRS.GD174.1456]

MCRAE, ALEXANDER, from Inverness, graduated MA from King's College, Aberdeen, on 26 April 1813. [KCA]

MCRAE, ALEXANDER, master of the Active of Fort William trading with Inverness in 1827. [NRS.E504.17.9]

MCRAE, ANN, from Kilmorack, with Duncan [born 1796], Margaret [born 1797], and Farquhar [born 1799], emigrated via Fort William aboard the Sarah of Liverpool bound for Pictou, Nova Scotia, in June 1801. [NRS.RH2.4.87]

MCRAE, BETSEY, from Strathglass, emigrated via Fort William aboard the Sarah of Liverpool bound for Pictou, Nova Scotia, in June 1801. [NRS.RH2.4.87]

MCRAE, CHRISTOPHER, a Lieutenant of the Royal African Corps, testament, 28 February 1818, Com. Inverness. [NRS]

MCRAE, DUNCAN, born 17 March 1769 in Inverness-shire, died in North Carolina on 10 February 1837. [Cross Creek gravestone, Cumberland County, N.C.]

MCRAE, DUNCAN, Principal Coast Officer in Inverness in 1845. [NRS.CE7.18.6]

MCRAE, FINLAY, a shipowner in Beauly, 1850. [NRS.CS280.36.95]

MCRAE, MALCOLM, born 1800, son of Malcolm McRae the kirk officer in Glen Elg, was accused of assault in 1824. [NRS.AD14.24.87]

MCRAE, MARY, from Kilmorack, with Murdoch [born1794], emigrated via Fort William aboard the Sarah of Liverpool bound for Pictou, Nova Scotia, in June 1801. [NRS.RH2.4.87]

MACRAE, MURDO, born 1796, died 9 June 1884, husband of Margaret McDonald, born 1812, died 13 March 1881, parents of Charles MacRae and Donald MacRae merchants in Inverness. [Old High gravestone, Inverness]

MCSWEEN, FINLEY, born in Inverness-shire around 1746, died at Little Lynch's Creek, South Carolina, in 1829. [Camden Journal, 17.10.1829]

MCTAVISH, DONALD, born in Stratherick, [Srath Fhairgeag], emigrated to Canada, partner in the North West Company, an explorer and trader, drowned in River Columbia at Cape Disappointment, Oregon, on 22 May 1815. [DCB][AJ.3535][GM.85.376][NSRG.20.12.1815]

MCTAVISH, D., from Inverness, father of a son born in Ness Side, Haldimand township, Canada West, in 1843. [AJ.5016]

MCTAVISH, JOHN, a solicitor in Inverness, 1823. [NRS.CS271201]

MACTHOMAIS, JOHN, tacksman of Mid Guisachan, with his wife Jean Chisholm, and family, emigrated to Nova Scotia in 1821. [HOFL.679]

MCVICAR, KATHERINE, a thief, who was sentenced in Inverness on 27 April 1789 to be transported for life. [AJ.2156]

MANFORD, MARGARET, died at Fort George on 4 March 1854, Jane R. Scott Manford died there on 23 April 1865, and their brother William Manford who drowned in Hobson's Bay, Australia, on 9 September 1864. [Kirkton of Ardersier gravestone]

MANFORD, WILLIAM, born 1770, barrack master and Ordnance Storekeeper of Fort George, died there on 10 August 1833. [Kirkton of Ardersier gravestone]

MARTIN, CHARLES, born 1807, a surgeon, son of Alexander Martin a civil engineer in Inverness-shire, son-in-law of Dr Skinner in Pictou, Nova Scotia, died there on 10 September 1841. [AJ.4894][EEC.20277]

MARTIN, JOHN, born 1781 in Inch, died in Puslinch, Canada, on 12 January 1857. [EEC.21030]

MARTIN, MATTHEW TOWNSEND, MA, in Inverness, graduated MD from King's College, Aberdeen, on 21 October 1820. [KCA]

MASON, ARCHIBALD, overseer at Port Clair, parish of Boleskine and Abertarf, testament, 30 November 1799, Comm.Inverness. [NRS]

MASSON, JAMES, born 1805, farmer in Ballinreich, died 17 March 1873. [Brachlich gravestone]

MATHESON, ALEXANDER MARTIN, born in Kilmuir, Skye, of McEwan and Company in Victoria, Hong Kong, died in Macao on 9 August 1845. [AJ.5107]

MATHESON, ANGUS, born 1790, died 7 June 1858, his wife Margaret, born 1801, died 1858, both from Inverness-shire. [Little Narrows gravestone, Victoria, NS]

MATHESON, DUNCAN, son of John Matheson, settled in Demerara by 1844. [Struy, Inverness, gravestone]

MATHESON, FARQUHAR, son of John Matheson and his wife Flora MacRae in Inverness, emigrated to Canada, was killed at Fort Wellington, Upper Canada, on 7 November 1813. [HOM]

MATHESON, JOHN, son of Donald Matheson, [1744-1845], miller at Fernaig, parish schoolmaster at Lochalsh from 1820 to 1830, then emigrated to Cape Breton. [HOM]

MATHIESON, JOHN, from Inverness, graduated MA from King's College, Aberdeen, in March 1828, later minister at Ardesier. [KCA]

MATHESON, JOHN, son of John Matheson, settled in Demerara by 1844. [Struy, Inverness, gravestone]

MATHESON, Reverend JOHN, born 1808, Free Church minister of Ardersier, died 12 November 1848. [Kirkton of Ardersier gravestone]

MATHIESON, MARGARET, from Inverness, died in Georgetown, Demerara, on 27 July 1841. [AJ.4890]

MATHESON, RODERICK, born 1792 in Inverness, son of John Matheson and his wife Flora MacRae, emigrated to Canada before 1812, Paymaster of the Glengarry Fencibles from 1812 until 1816, as a military settler he was granted land in Upper Canada in 1816, settled in Perth, Lanark, died 1873. [HOM][PAO]

MATHESON, RODERICK, born 1814, son of John Matheson, settled in Demerara, died on 20 February 1884. [Struy, Inverness, gravestone]

MATHIESON, WILLIAM, master of the Industry of Inverness trading with Newcastle in 1813. [NRS.E504.17.8]

MAY, GEORGE, son of Andrew May a writer in Inverness, a student at Marischal College, Aberdeen, in 1820. [MCA]

MAY, JOHN, son of Andrew May in Inverness, a student at Marischal College, Aberdeen, in 1830. [MCA]

MELROSE, ALEXANDER, a merchant in Fort William, sequestration, 1850. [NRS.CS280.36.86]

MELROSE, ELIZABETH, born 1832 in Inverness-shire, wife of Joseph Campbell, died at 20 North Oxford Street, Brooklyn, New York, on 23 June 1871. [S.8733]

MELVILLE, ROBERT, a merchant and fish curer, also Captain of the Volunteer Corps in Ullapool, was charged with obstructing an Exciseman in 1802, was fined 300 merks. [NRS.JC11.40]

MICHAEL, JOHN, master of the Janet of Fort William trading with Inverness in 1823. [NRS.E504.17.9]

MILLER, JAMES, alias Hector Cameron, born in Inverness, a deserter from the 3rd Battalion of the Rifle Brigade, was accused of theft in 1816. [NRS.AD14.16.60]

MILLER, JAMES, Customs Controller in Inverness in 1849, Customs Controller and Surveyor in Inverness in 1852. [NRS.CE7.18.18]

MILLER, ROBERT, master of the Kitty of Inverness who was lost at sea in October 1858. [Chapel Yard gravestone, Inverness]

MILLER SIMON, a butcher in Inverness, testament, 16 January 1790, Comm. Inverness. [NRS]

MILNE, FORBES, born 1784 in Inverness, a gamekeeper now a pauper in Culcabock in 1857, father of William Forbes a servant in America, etc. [IPR]

MILNE, JAMES, master of the John Alexander of Inverness in 1824. [NRS.E504.17.9]

MITCHELL, ANDREW, born 1753 in Inverness, 'for many years a resident of this city', died on 3 May 1826. [Unitarian Church, Charleston, South Carolina]

MITCHELL, HENRY LUMSDEN, son of Henry Mitchell in Badenoch, graduate MA from Marischal College, Aberdeen, in 1857, later a Church of Scotland chaplain in Ceylon. [MCA]

MITCHELL, HENRY, born 1830, a chemist in Inverness, died on 19 January 1911., husband of Jessie MacDonald, born 1831, died 22 December 1923. [Old High gravestone, Inverness]

MITCHELL, JAMES, from Inverness, graduated MA from King's College, Aberdeen, in March 1836. [KCA]

MITCHELL, KENNETH, a cooper in Old Town, Aigas, Kilmorack, was accused of theft in 1812. [NRS.AD14.12.35]

MITCHELL, THOMAS, son of John Mitchell in Inverness-shire, a student at Marischal College, Aberdeen, in 1830. [MCA]

MITCHEL, WILLIAM, son of William Mitchel in Kilmanivaig, a student in Marischal College around 1800. [MCA]

MITCHELL, WILLIAM, a tenant in Gordonhall, Kingussie, papers, 1813-1827. [NRS.GD44.28.7]

MOFFAT, JAMES, in Kinlochishart, Strath, a victim of goat thieves in 1837. [NRS.AD14.37.18]

MOIR, JOHN, born 1785, a millwright in Inverness, died 7 January 1832, husband of Margaret, parents of James Moir a linen merchant in Inverness, born 1831, died 9 January 1855. [Chapel Yard gravestone, Inverness]

MONRO, DANIEL, son of Reverend Daniel Monro in Inverness, a student at Marischal College, Aberdeen, in 1837, later minister at Inch. [MCA]

MONRO, GEORGE, son of James Monro in Inverness, was educated at Marischal College around 1815. [MCA]

MONRO, JAMES, born 1811, son of James Monro in Pictou, Nova Scotia – late of Inverness, died in Pictou on 14 August 1841. [AJ.4887]

MORISON, PETER, son of Allan Morison in the Kirkton of Glenelg, was accused of stealing goats in 1837. [NRS.AD14.37.18]

MORRISON, SKENE, born 1803, died 25 August 1832, husband of Elizabeth Gellion, born 1806, died 11 August 1879. [Chapel Yard gravestone, Inverness]

MORRISON, WILLIAM, born 1825, a mariner in Merkinch, Inverness, died on 21 March 1896, husband of Jane MacQuillian, born 1825, died on 20 September 1885. [Chapel Yard gravestone, Inverness]

MULLINGS, Mrs ANN, born 1793 in Inverness, widow of Captain John Mullings, a resident of Charleston, South Carolina, for 60 years, died there on 1 January 1874. [Old Scots gravestone, Charleston]

MUNRO, ALEXANDER, an apprentice of James Lyon in Inverness, guilty of theft, sentenced to two months imprisonment in 1810. [NRS.JC11.51]

MUNRO, ANN, wife of Adam Hood a house-wright in Inverness, died 27 June 1843. [NRS.S/H]

MUNRO, CHRISTIAN, wife of Duncan Grant a cooper in Inverness, dead by 1864. [NRS.S/H]

MUNRO, COLIN, late of Grenada, died in Inverness on 18 October 1823. [DPCA.1108]

MUNRO, DONALD, from Glen Urquhart, emigrated to Pictou, Nova Scotia, in 1818, settled at Big Cove, Merigomish. [TGS.53.448]

MUNRO, DONALD, born 1821, died at Clephanton on 5 October 1895. [Brachlich gravestone]

MUNRO, FARQUHAR, born 1820, son of Farquhar Munro, [1776-1840], and his wife Margaret Sutherland, [1776-1847], died in Akland Village, Cape of Good Hope, South Africa, on 25 December 1850. [Old High Church gravestone, Inverness]

MUNRO, HUGH, born 1796, a seaman, died 3 January 1876, husband of Eliza Carstairs, born 1797, died 22 September 1872, grandparents of William M. Munro in Pictou, Nova Scotia. [Chapel Yard gravestone, Inveness]

MUNRO, JOHN, with his wife Rebecca Cumming and family, from Glen Urquhart, emigrated to Pictou, Nova Scotia, in 1820, settled at Moose River. [TGS.53.448]

MUNRO, JOHN, born 1792, a house-carpenter in Inverness, died 22 August 1866. [Chapel Yard gravestone, Inverness]

MUNRO, JOHN, born 1 May 1800, a dyer in Inverness, died 15 July 1879, husband of Isabella MacBean, born July 1800, died 6 February 1888. [Chapel Yard gravestone, Inverness]

MUNRO, MARY, eldest daughter of James Munro formerly in Inverness, married James Grant a merchant, in Pictou, Nova Scotia, on 15 September 1831. [AJ.4378]

MURCAR, THOMAS, born 1766, a pensioner, died 1818, husband of Charlotte Ferrier, born 1764, died 1848. [Brachlich gravestone]

MURDOCH, or CAMPBELL, ANN, born 1802 in Boleskine and Abertaff, a widow, servant and pauper in King Street, Inverness, in 1857. [IPR]

NAIRN, WILLIAM, born 1790 in Inverness-shire, a servant to Robert Lyon, with his wife born 1794, and children James born 1816, Margaret born 1824, Charlotte born 187, and William born 1829, from Inverness-shire, settled in the Swan River Colony, Australia, in 1830. [BPP.3.438]

NICHOLSON, ALEXANDER, born 1780 on Skye, died on Prince Edward Island on 26 September 1820. [Polly gravestone, Belfast, PEI]

NICHOLSON, E. M., born 1795, son of Robert Nicholson, a Captain of the 55th Regiment, died in Madras, India, on9 August 1831. [Chapel Yard gravestone, Inverness]

NICHOLSON, JOHN, from Inverness, graduated MA from King's College, Aberdeen, on 30 March 1810, later minister at Steinscholl. [KCA]

NICHOLSON, MALCOLM, born 1750 in Inverness, died in Halifax, Nova Scotia, on 29 March 1838. [Acadian Recorder, 31.3.1838]

NICHOLSON, ROBERT, born 1758, Staff Adjutant of Inverness, died 12 June 1818. [Chapel Yard gravestone, Inverness]

NICHOLSON, ROBERT, born 1789 son of Robert Nicholson, a Lieutenant of the 78th Regiment who died in Goa, India, on 26 November 1810. [Chapel Yard gravestone, Inverness]

NICOL, ALEXANDER, born 1748, a cartwright burgess of Inverness, died on 3 March 1816, husband of Mary Fraser, born 1761, died 9 May 1833. [Chapel Yard gravestone, Inverness]

NICOL, JAMES, son of John Nicol in Kiltarlity, graduated MA from Marischal College, Aberdeen, in 1807. [MCA]

NICOL, ROBERT, born 1797 in Inverness, formerly in Jamaica, died in Inverness on 27 February 1844. [Chapel Yard gravestone, Inverness]

NICOLSON, WILLIAM, born 1814, in Stuarton, Ardesier, died 15 November 1885. [Brachlich gravestone]

NOBLE, ALEXANDER, from Inverness, graduated MA from King's College, Aberdeen, on 27 March 1800, later schoolmaster at Glass. [KCA]

NOBLE, HUGH, alias Innes, born in Inverness, a deserter from the 3rd Battalion of the Rifle Brigade, was accused of theft in 1816. [NRS.AD14.16.60]

NOBLE, JOHN, born 1756, a dyer, and guild-brother of Inverness, died 16 April 1802, husband of Janet Robertson who died on 1 April 1833. [Chapel Yard gravestone, Inverness]

NOBLE, JOHN, from Inverness, graduated MA from King's College, Aberdeen, in March 1826, later Rector of Tain Academy, and minister of Fodderty, joined the Free Church. [KCA]

NOBLE, MARGARET, born 1792 in Daviot, a pauper in Huntly Street, Inverness, in 1857. [IPR]

OLIVER, ROBERT, in Cullachie, died 11 September 1823, husband of [1] Margaret Blaikie, born 1773, died 4 November 1797, and [2] Isabella Stewart died 23 August 1826. [Kilchuimen gravestones]

ORD, JOHN, chaplain to the garrison at Fort William, also Rector of Fort William Grammar School in 1811. [NRS.CC2.8.115.2]

PACKMAN, CHARLES, in Uchnachan, Kilmonivaig, a victim of theft in 1824. [NRS.AD14.24.84]

PARK, CHARLES, from Inverness, died in Hamilton, Canada West, on 6 March 1859. [CM.21497]

PARK, JOSEPH, born 1832, lock-keeper at Fort Augustus, died 28 May 1881. [Kilchuimen gravestone]

PATERSON, ALEXANDER, from Inverness, graduated MA from King's College, Aberdeen, in March 1846, later a Free Church minister in Dunblane and Falkirk. [KCA]e

PATERSON, CHARLES, master of the Isabella of Inverness trading with Ballachulish in 1819. [NRS.E504.17.8]

PATERSON, ISAAC, born 1798 in Inverness-shire, with his wife Anne, born 1805 in Ross-shire, emigrated via Liverpool to America, naturalised in New York on 30 October 1823. [N.Y. Court of Common Pleas]

PATTERSON, JOHN, in Inverness, applied to settle in Canada on 30 August 1827. [TNA.CO384.5.105]

PATTERSON, JOHN, born 1801 in Inverness, a salmon fisher now a pauper in 38 Huntly Street, Inverness, in 1857, husband of Catherine, born 1801 at Tummel Bridge, parents of John Patterson born 1833, a carrier possibly in New York. [IPR]

PATERSON, MARGARET, daughter of Robert Paterson from Inverness, married George Rome from Annan, Dumfries-shire, in Brooklyn, New York, on 15 March 1870. [AO]

PATERSON, PETER, a Lieutenant of the Inverness Militia, a letter to Lady Grant in 1804. [NRS.GD248.194.3/43]

PATIENCE, DANIEL, master of the Macduff of Inverness trading with Newcastle in 1821, and with Archangel, Russia, in 1827. [NRS.E504.17.8/9]

RANKIN, ALEXANDER, his wife and two children, from Carnach, Glen Coe, emigrated via Fort William aboard the Friends of Saltcoats master John How to Montreal in July 1802. [GkAd.59]

RANKINE, THOMAS, from Inverness, graduated MA from King's College, Aberdeen, on 29 March 1805. [KCA]

REID, ANDREW, born 1832 in Inverness, son of Angus Reid, a tailor, and his wife Catherine Treasurer, a pauper in Meal Market Close, Inverness, in 1857. [IPR]

REID, CHARLES, Principal Coast Officer of Inverness in 1834. [NRS.CE7.18.5]

REID, DANIEL, tenant of Ellanreach, versus Roderick MacRae in the Kirkton of Glen Elg in 1837. [NRS.CS46.1837.2.36]

REID, GEORGE, master of the Caledonia of Fort William trading with Fort William in 1812.   [NRS.E504.17.8]

REID, JAMES, master of the Inverness of Inverness trading with Easdale in 1820. [NRS.E504.17.8]

REID, JOHN, in Tobago, son and heir of John Reid a feuar in Urquhart, 1796. [NRS.S/H]

REID, WILLIAM, in Glen Elg, 1817. [NRS.SEQNS.R2.13]

RHIND, DUNCAN, born 1778 in Dores, a widower, gardener, and pauper in Chapel Street, Inverness in 1857. [IPR]

RITCHIE, or FRASER, JANET, born 1798 in Dores, a servant now a pauper in Lochgorm in 1857. [IPR]

RITCHIE, JOHN, son of Alexander Ritchie a farmer at Lochgorin, Inverness, was accused of murder in 1807. [NRS.JC11.48]

ROBERTSON, ALEXANDER, born 1772, an innkeeper at Kenlochunigan, died 30 March 1828. [Kilchuimen gravestone]

ROBERTSON, ALEXANDER, [1831-1905], father of Alexander H. Robertson, born 1862, died in New York on 30 April 1897. [Urquhart gravestone]

ROBERTSON, ALEXANDER, a farmer in Canada West, son and heir of Donald Robertson a tenant farmer in Dalreich, who died on 22 May 1859. [NRS.S/H]

ROBERTSON, ANN, born 1807 in Inverness, a servant now a pauper in Celt Street, Inverness, in 1857. [IPR]

ROBERTSON, ARTHUR JOHN, in Inches, Inverness, married Marianne Pattinson, daughter of Richard Pattinson, from Upper Canada, in Glasgow on 13 March 1824. [DPCA.1131]

ROBERTSON, DONALD, a tenant farmer in Dalriach, died 22 May 1859, father of Alexander Robertson a farmer in Canada West. [NRS.S/H]

ROBERTSON, FARQUHAR, tacksman of Scalasaig, Glen Elg, emigrated with his wife Katherine McLeod to Canada in 1823. [TML]

ROBERTSON, HARRY, born 19 July 1776 in Kiltearn, son of Reverend Harry Robertson and his wife Anne Forbes, died in Demerara in 1795. [F.7.43]

ROBERTSON, ISAAC, born 1798 in Inverness-shire, wife Anne, born 1805 in Ross-shire, emigrated via Liverpool to America, naturalised in New York on 30 October 1823. [NARA]

ROBERTSON, Dr JAMES, a physician in Inverness, married Katherine Inglis, daughter of the late Alexander Inglis in South Carolina, in Edinburgh on 20 October 1794. [GM.64.1148]

ROBERTSON, JAMES, in Balnacraig, Kingussie, was accused of maliciously attacking and invading inhabited dwellings in 1845. [NRS.AD14.4.122]

ROBERTSON, JESS or JANET, born 1818 in Inverness, a pauper in Celt Street, Inverness, in 1857. [IPR]

ROBERTSON, JOHN, son of Alan Robertson a gentleman in Inverness, graduated MA from Marischal College, Aberdeen, in 1804, an advocate in Aberdeen by 1810. [MCA]

ROBERTSON, MARY FRASER, daughter of Captain Robertson in Inverness, married Roderick Matheson, late paymaster of the Glengarry Light Infantry, in Montreal on 5 November 1823. [Fife Herald, 132]

ROBERTSON, RACHAEL CUTHBERT, eldest daughter of Captain Robertson of the Inverness Militia, married David Chisholme, an attorney at law, in Montreal on 16 May 1822. [BM.12.518]

ROBERTSON, WILLIAM, son of Alan Robertson a gentleman in Inverness, a student in Marischal College around 1800. [MCA]

ROBERTSON, WILLIAM, a former member of the Inverness Militia, emigrated with his wife and daughter, as a military settler he was granted land in Bathurst, Upper Canada, in 1832. [PAO]

ROSE, ALEXANDER, born 1738 in Inverness, emigrated to America before 1755, a merchant in Virginia and North Carolina, married Eunice Lea on 5 May 1774, died in Person County, N.C. [RSA] [INC]

ROSE, CATHERINE, daughter of John Rose of Holm, and wife of Captain George Easton of the 35th Regiment, died in Guadaloupe on 29 May 1794. [SM.56.588]

ROSE, CHARLES, his wife Catherine McBean, and children, from Croy and Dalcross, Inverness-shire, settled in the Scotch Settlement, Columbiana County, Ohio, in 1804. [WRHS.VFC.1247]

ROSE, CHARLES, from Inverness, graduated MA from King's College, Aberdeen, on 26 April 1813, later schoolmaster in Rosskeen. [KCA]

ROSE, DAVID, born 1792, corn merchant in Inverness, died 3 February 1881, husband of Sarah Ormiston, born 1793, died on 18 August 1835. [Chapel Yard gravestone, Inverness]

ROSE, or MCLEAN, EUPHEMIA, born 1778 in Inverness, an outdoor servant now a pauper at Culloden Mains in 1857. [IPR]

ROSE, MARGARET, born 1777 in Daviot, a servant now a pauper at 20 Gilbert Street, Inverness, in 1857. [IPR]

ROSE, ROBERT, a merchant in Inverness, testament, 6 November 1790, Comm. Inverness. [NRS]

ROSS, ALEXANDER, from Inverness, graduated MA from King's College, Aberdeen, on 26 April 1813, later minister in Ullapool. [KCA]

ROSS, or MCFARQUHAR, ALEXANDER, a prisoner in Inverness Tolbooth, found guilty of stealing sheep, was sentenced to transportation for seven years in 1817. [NRS.JC11.58]

ROSS, ALEXANDER, a gardener in Glen Urquhart, emigrated to Nova Scotia in 1818, settled at Sunny Brae. [TGS.53.458]

ROSS, ALEXANDER, son of James Ross in Inverness-shire, was educated at Marischal College in Aberdeen from 1847, graduate MB in 1853. [MCA]

ROSS, ALEXANDER, son of John Ross in Glen Urquhart, emigrated to Pictou, Nova Scotia, in 1818, settled at East River. [TGS.53.455]

ROSS, ALEXANDER, in Unachan, Kilmonivaig, was accused of assault, outlawed in 1837. [NRS.AD14.37.1; JC26.1837.70]

ROSS, ANNIE, born 1792 in Daviot, a servant now a pauper in King Street, Inverness, in 1857. [IPR]

ROSS, CHARLES, son of Reverend Thomas Ross in Kilmonivaig, a student in Marischal College in 1790s. [MCA]

ROSS, CHARLES, born 1786, a merchant and burgess of Inverness, died 16 December 1851, husband of Margaret Chisholm. [Chapel Yard gravestone, Inverness]

ROSS, CHARLES, from Kincraig, emigrated to Canada, an employee of the Hudson Bay Company from 1818 until his death at Fort Victoria on 27 June 1844. [HBRS]

ROSS, COLIN, born 1820 in Inverness, settled in Montreal, died in Quebec on 12 June 1846. [AJ.5140]

ROSS, DONALD, in Broulan, Kilmorack, accused of sheep stealing in 1812. [NRS.AD14.12.48]

ROSS, Mrs ELIZABETH, born 1808 in Kirkhill, Inverness-shire, wife of John Ross of the Necropolis, died in Toronto, Canada, on 19 December 1852. [W.xiii.1293]

ROSS, GEORGE, merchant in Inverness, died 29 October 1835, husband of Elizabeth Fraser, born 1784, died 12 July 1857. [Chapel Yard gravestone, Inverness]

ROSS, HENRY, master mason of Fort George, died 30 December 1837, husband of E. McKenzie who died in 1824. [Kirkton of Ardersier gravestone]

ROSS, HUGH, born 1797 in Inverness-shire, emigrated to Nova Scotia in 1813, and a theological student at Pictou Academy on Prince Edward Island from 1820 to 1824, minister at Cape Breton and in Nova Scotia from 1827 until 1858, husband of Flora McKay, [1798-1874], died on 1 December 1858. [F.1.622][HPC]

ROSS, HUGH, born 1772 in Rosskeen, a labourer and a soldier now a pauper in Ross's Close, Inverness, in 1857. [IPR]

ROSS, JAMES, Inverlochy, Kirkmichael, was accused of beating and wounding officers of the Revenue in 1818, outlawed. [NRS.JC11.58]

ROSS, JAMES, born 1796, a merchant and grocer in Drumillie, Duthil, was accused of murder in 1826. [NRS.AD14.26.126]

ROSS, JOHN, acting Customs Controller at the Port of Inverness, 1820s. [NRS.E504.17.8]

ROSS, JOHN, born 1 March 1824, son of John Ross, [1799-1866], in Carrbridge, and his wife Matilda Fraser, died in Redbank, Victoria, Australia, on 7 July 1861. [Duthil gravestone]

ROSS, MARY, widow of John Beaton a labourer at Fort George, accused of theft in 1817. [NRS.AD14.17.40]

ROSS, PATRICK, born 1823, son of Reverend Thomas Ross in Kilmonivaig, [Cill Mo Naomhaig], died in Chicago, Illinois, on 31 December 1863. [Laggan gravestone]

ROSS, ROBERT, of the 4th Royal Irish Dragoon Guards, married Miss C. H. MacBean, only child of Aeneas MacBean of Tomatin and St Thomas, in Inverness on 7 April 1819. [EA.5778.233]

ROSS, Reverend THOMAS, minister of Kilmonivaig, letters, 1787-1810. [NRS.GD128.19.13]

ROSS, THOMAS, son of Evan Ross in Kilmonivaig, a student at Marischal College, Aberdeen, in 1840s, later in Torandush near Fort Augustus, then a merchant in Bombay, India. [MCA]

ROSS, WILLIAM, born 1788, son of John Ross in Achadhtubhaidh, Urquhart, with his wife and children, emigrated to Pictou, Nova Scotia, in 1818, died on 7 December Invernahyle, [Inbhir na h-Aidhle], died in New York during 1813. [Stewarts of Appin]

ROSS, WILLIAM, tidesman at Portmahomack in 1816. [NRS.E504.17.8]

ROSS, WILLIAM, born 1854, a baker in Beauly, died in Providence, USA, on 24 April 1901, his wife Sarah McKenzie, born 1848, died on 22 January 1881. [Beauly Priory gravestone]

ROY, ROBERT, from Inverness, graduated MA from King's College, Aberdeen, on 25 March 1814, later a Writer to the Signet. [KCA]

RUSSELL, ELIZA, a widow in Telford Street, Inverness, a victim of theft and fraud in 1846. [NRS.JC26.1847.637]

SCOTT, ALEXANDER, from Urquhart, emigrated via Fort William aboard the Friends of Saltcoats master John How to Montreal in July 1802. [GkAd.59] [CMM]

SCOTT, DAVID, barrack master of Fort Augustus, testamentary papers, 1795-1801. [NRS.GD23.7.30]

SCOTT, DONALD, with his wife, Alexander Scott, Duncan Scott, Janet Scott, and two children, from Aberchalder, emigrated via Fort William aboard the Friends of Saltcoats master John How to Montreal in July 1802. [GkAd.59]

SCOTT, JAMES, in Kingussie, granted a bond of cation for Alexander McDonald in Cattil Lodge, Kingussie, in 1817. [NRS.CS271.676]

SEBASTIAN, SAMUEL, born 1828 in Inverness, emigrated to America in 1848, a declaration of intent to naturalise on 17 January 1856 in Norfolk County Court, Virginia. [VSA]

SHARP, WILLIAM, a stationer and bookbinder in Inverness, testament, 4 August 1797, Comm. Inverness. [NRS]

SHAW, ALEXANDER, a merchant in Inverness, testament, 30 January 1794, Comm. Inverness. [NRS]

SHAW, ALEXANDER, born 1803, his wife Marion born 1814, son Alexander born 1846, and son John born 1850, from Portree, Skye, emigrated via Liverpool aboard the Thames bound for Melbourne, Australia, on 3 November 1852. [NRS.HD4/5],

SHAW, ALEXANDER, [1790-1863], a farmer at Clune, father of John Shaw, born 22 February 1825, an architect who died at Meridon Hill, USA, on 11 October 1861. [Dores gravestone]

SHAW, DONALD, a messenger in Inverness, testament, 8 September 1790, Comm. Inverness. [NRS]

SHAW, JAMES, born 1822 in Abernethy, a storekeeper who was naturalised in Charleston, South Carolina, on 5 April 1853. [NARA.M1183.1]

SHAW, JOHN, born 1749, farmer in Pollphatan, died in January 1826, husband of Elizabeth McIntosh, born 1767, died in January 1838. [Brachlich gravestone]

SHAW, SUSAN GORDON, only child of Captain A. Shaw in Dalnavert, [Dail nam Feart], Inverness, married George Kinghorn Prince, MD, of Aqualta Vale, St Mary, Jamaica, in Port Antonio, Jamaica, on 23 April 1826, [EA.6534.437]; died at Aqualta Vale on 9 December 1826. [BM.21.773]

SHAW, THOMAS, in Keppoch, a tack of the Mains of Dalnavert, Alvie, for nineteen years in 1804. [NRS.GD176.1436]

SIM, WALTER, born 1809 in Invergordon, a porter now a pauper in Inverness, 1857. [IPR]

SIMPSON, ISABELLA, born 1804 in Inverness, a servant now a pauper in Castle Street, Inverness, in 1857. [IPR]

SINCLAIR, ALLAN, from Urquhart, was educated at King's College, Aberdeen, in 1842, later a minister at Kenmore. [KCA]

SINCLAIR, JOHN, from Culloden, Inverness-shire, later in Nova Scotia, heir to Donald MacPherson a farmer in Balchree of Petty, later Blarnaphat, Inverness-shire, 1851. [NRS.S/H]

SINCLAIR, MALCOLM, a merchant in Fort William, edict of executry, 1812. [NRS.CC2.8.116.2]

SINCLAIR, MARGARET, daughter of Hector Sinclair, married John Robertson from Toronto, Canada, in Petty on 25 March 1841. [AJ.4866]

SINCLAIR, Sir ROBERT, of Murkle, testament, 7 March 1796, Comm/H]. Inverness. [NRS]

SINCLAIR, WILLIAM, from Kirkhill, was educated at King's College, Aberdeen, in 1844, later a minister at Lochalsh. [KCA]

SMITH, ALEXANDER, born 1782, tacksman of Bona Ferry, died 8 October 1835. [Dores gravestone]

SMITH, DONALD, a merchant in Inverness, testament, 19 February 1799, Comm. Inverness. [NRS]

SMITH, DONALD, master of the <u>Lady Margaret of Fort William</u> trading between Ballachulish and Inverness in 1822. [NRS.E504.17.9]

SMITH, DONALD, in Cambridge, USA, son and heir of James Smith a farm servant in Inverness, 1842. [NRS.S/H]

SMITH, JAMES, son of Reverend William Smith in Petty, graduated MA from Marischal College, Aberdeen, in 1795, later minister of Urquhart and Glenmoriston, [MCA]

SMITH, JOHN, son of John Smith an architect in Inverness, was educated at Marischal College, Aberdeen, in 1844. [MCA]

SMITH, LAUGHLAN, from Inverness, a soldier in Wolfe's Army at the taking of Quebec, Seigneur of St Denis and La Pocatirre, 'upwards of 100 years of age', died in Quebec on 29 June 1823. [S.380.360][EA]

SMITH, NEIL, from Inverness, graduated MA from King's College, Aberdeen, on 30 March 1801. [KCA]

SINCLAIR, MARGARET, daughter of Hector Sinclair in Kerroward, married John Robertson from Toronto, Canada, in Petty, Inverness-shire, on 25 March 1841. [AJ.4866]

SMITH, DAVID, born 1793, a shoemaker in Inverness, died 15 March 1840, husband of Margaret Ferrier. [Chapel Yard gravestone, Inverness]

SMITH, JAMES, a farm servant in Inverness, dead by 1842, father of Donald Smith in Cambridge, USA. [NRS.S/H]

SMITH, JANET, born 1790 in Inverness, a servant now a pauper in Bisset Close, Inverness, in 1857. [IPR]

SMITH, JOHN, son of John Smith an architect in Inverness, was educated at Marischal College in Aberdeen in 1844. [MCA]

SMITH, JOHN, born 1780 in Inverness, a weaver now a pauper in Celt Street, Inverness, in 1857. [IPR]

SMITH, NEIL, from Inverness, graduated MA from King's College, Aberdeen, on 30 March 1801, later minister in

SMITH, ROBERT, a clothier in Inverness, 1831. [NRS.GD23.5.394]

STALKER, JOHN, born 1750 in Inverness, died at the Clyde River, Nova Scotia, on 29 August 1834. [Halifax Journal.15.9.1834]

STEEL, DONALD, in 'Charlotte Town in America' in a letter to Major Ranald MacDonald of Staffa, states that he 'wishes to come home; false reports delude emigrants; objects to climate and low wages', dated 16 September 1802. [NRS.GD248.671.6/9]

STEPHEN, JOHN, born 1767, a flaxdresser, died in 1847, husband of Ann McDonald, born 1775, died in 1861. [Chapel Yard gravestone, Inverness]

STEWART, ALEXANDER, a goldsmith in Inverness from 1796 to 1812. [Inverness Library]

STEWART, ALEXANDER, with one child, from Fort Augustus, emigrated via Fort William aboard the Friends of Saltcoats master John How to Montreal in July 1802. [GkAd.59]

STEWART, ALEXANDER, son of Robert Stewart a mason in Inch, Kingussie, was accused of maliciously attacking and invading inhabited dwellings in 1845. [NRS.AD14.4.122]

STEWART, ALEXANDER, born 1791, of Windmill, Inverness, died 13 June 1868, husband of Christian Murison, born 1810, died 4 September 1899. [Chapel Yard gravestone, Inverness]

STEWART, ALEXANDER, born 1798 on Skye, died on Prince Edward Island on 27 February 1890. [Little Sands gravestone, PEI]; his wife Catherine, born 1813 on Skye, died on P.E.I. on 6 February 1883. [Little Sands gravestone, PEI]

STEWART, Lieutenant Colonel late of the North Carolina Highlanders, died at Invernahyce on 2 Aril 1793. [GM.63.378]

STEWART, CATHERINE, born 1776 in Inverness, a servant now a pauper in Bank Street, Inverness, in 1857. [IPR]

STEWART, CHARLES, from Fort George, was educated at Marischal College, Aberdeen, in 1847, later a minister in Bannockburn. [MCA]

STEWART, DUGALD, in Fort William, dead by 1858, father of John Stewart in Jamaica. [NRS.S/H]

STEWART, DUNCAN, the Customs Collector of New London, Connecticut, from 1764, a Loyalist in 1776, settled at Fort William, Inverness-shire, by 1788. [TNA.AO12.104.40] [NLS.CH3848]

STEWART, Mrs ISABELLA, born 1789 in Inverness-shire, emigrated to Nova Scotia in 1801, died 21 April 1866, wife of Peter Stewart born 1787, died 1832. [Creighton gravestone, Pictou, NS]

STEWART, JAMES, Lieutenant Governor of Fort George, testament, 1809. [NRS.GD23.7.38]

STEWART, JAMES, born 1778, son of Andrew Stewart in Invernahyle, husband of Isabella Tod, parents of David Stewart, died in New York in 1813. [SAE]

STEWART, or MACDONALD, JEAN, born 1789 in Contin, a servant now a pauper and a widow in Huntly Street, Inverness, in 1857, mother of Alexander, born 1821, a coachmaker who settled in Australia. [IPR]

STEWART, JOHN, born 1769, a plasterer in Castle Street, Inverness, died on 19 January 1837, his wife Margaret Crawford McKenzie, died on 25 December 1844. [Chapel Yard gravestone, Inverness]

STEWART, JOHN, Mary Stewart, Catherine Stewart, from Boline, emigrated via Fort William aboard the <u>Friends of Saltcoats</u> master John How to Montreal in July 1802. [GkAd.59]

STEWART, JOHN, in Jamaica, later in Fort William, Inverness-shire, son and heir of Dugald Stewart in Fort William, 1858. [NRS.S/H]

STEWART, JOHN, born 1841, died 28 February 1890. [Brachlich gravestone]

STEWART, LACHLIN, born 1819, a shoemaker, died 24 April 1860, husband of Elspet Winks, born 1818, died 1855. [Old High gravestone, Inverness]

STEWART, RONALD D., born 1827 on Skye, died on Prince Edward Island on 15 October 1896. [Little Sands gravestone, PEI]

STEWART, WILLIAM, born 1746, a weaver burgess of Inverness, died in November 1822, husband of Lusci McIntosh, born 1756, died in February 1825. [Chapel Yard gravestone, Inverness]

STEWART, WILLIAM, a solicitor in Inverness, letters, 1848. [NRS.GD248.623.9]

STEWART, Mrs, wife of Duncan Stewart of Achnacoan the Customs Collector at Fort William, died at Stronchrigan on 31 May 1820. [SM.86.190]

STRACHAN, DONALD, born 1800, died at Aldourie on 26 May 1850, husband of Katherine MacDonald, born 1804, died 10 August 1876. [Dores gravestone]

STRACHAN, JOHN, born 1783, a house carpenter in Inverness, husband of Sophia Robertson, died 20 October 1853. [Old High gravestone, Inverness]

STRATHEARN, EDWARD, born 10 April 1814 in Inverness, died in Brussels, Belgium, on 21 August 1879. [Old High Church, Inverness]

STRONACH, GEORGE, master of the Inverness of Inverness trading with Fort William in 1811. [NRS.E504.17.8]

SUTER, CATHERINE, born 1803, daughter of James Suter a merchant in Inverness, died there on 17 May 1820. [SM.86.96]

SUTER, JAMES, junior, master of the George of Inverness trading with Archangel, Russia, in1827. [NRS.E504.17.9]

SUTER, PETER, born 1791, son of James Suter a merchant in Inverness, an assistant surgeon of the Honourable East India Company, died in Calcutta, India, on 10 June 1821. [AJ.3857]

SUTHERLAND, ALEXANDER, from St Kilda, Inverness, married Mrs Elizabeth French, second daughter of William Ross in Huntly, Aberdeenshire, in Melbourne, Australia, on 19 August 1856. [AJ.5681]

SUTHERLAND, ANDREW, was granted a tack of Lairgindour and Baile Laggan, Strathnairn, for nineteen years in 1833. [NRS.GD176.1453]

SUTHERLAND, GEORGE, born 1764, died 10 October 1813, husband of Isabella MacKinzie, born 1770, died 26 January 1822. [Chapel Yard gravestone, Inverness]

SUTHERLAND, or MACKENZIE, JANET, born 1800 in Glen Urquhart, an outdoor labourer now a pauper in Davis Square, Inverness, in 1857. [IPR]

SYMON, JAMES, born 1791, a mason who died in Tobago on 5 July 1822. [Chapel Yard gravestone, Inverness]

TALLACH, THOMAS, from Inverness, graduated MA from King's College, Aberdeen, in March 1851. [KCA]

TAYLOR, ALEXANDER, born 1804, shipmaster in Inverness, died 23 December 1851. [Chapel Yard gravestone, Inverness]

TAYLOR, ALEXANDER, born 1833, master of the Lady Havelock died on passage from Liverpool to Quebec on 26 August 1872, buried in Quebec. [Chapel Yard gravestone, Inverness]

TAYLOR, DONALD, born 1784 in Inverness, a labourer now a pauper, in Duff Street, Inverness, 1857. [IPR]

THOMSON, ALEXANDER, with Bella McIntosh his wife, from Glen Urquhart, settled at Sunny Brae, Nova Scotia, in 1801. [TGS.53.458]

THOMSON, or ROSS, CATHERINE, born 1822 in Inverness, a house servant now a pauper and widow in Huntly Street, Inverness, 1857. [IPR]

THOMSON, HECTOR, tenant in Kilmorack, with Janet, and Simon [born 1798], emigrated via Fort William aboard the Sarah of Liverpool bound for Pictou, Nova Scotia, in June 1801. [NRS.RH2.4.87]

THOMSON, JOHN, from Glen Urquhart, settled at Sunny Brae, Nova Scotia, in 1801. [TGS.53.458]

TOLLANDS, or MCDONALD, MARY, born 1797 in Inverness, a maid servant now a pauper in 1857. [IPR]

TOLMIE, JOHN, born 1764, a farmer in Inverness, died 5 February 1827, husband of Symours Munro, born 1769, died 10 August 1799. [Chapel Yard gravestone, Inverness]

TOLMIE, MARGARET, born 1786 in Inverness, a servant now a pauper in Friar's Place, Inverness, in 1857. [IPR]

TOLMIE, THOMAS, a merchant in Inverness, testament, 25 February 1790, Comm. Inverness. [NRS]

TOMLINSON, THOMAS, born 1795, a horse dealer in King Street, Inverness, was accused of theft in 1825. [NRS.AD14.25.229]

TRAPAUD, ALEXANDER, Lieutenant Governor of Fort Augustus, testament, 21 April 1797, Comm. Inverness. [NRS]

TREASURER, or YOUNG, ELIZABETH, born 1780 in Dundee, a servant now a pauper in Muirtown Street, Inverness, in 1857. [IPR]

TULLOCH, ALEXANDER FRANCIS TANNACHIE, son of Francis Tulloch, formerly Major of the Inverness Militia, died in Jamaica on 23 March 1835. [GM.NS4.102]

TULLOCH, or MCINTOSH, CATHERINE, born 1784 in Inverness, a servant now a pauper in Haugh in 1857, mother of Jess in Australia. [IPR]

TULLOCH, DUNCAN, born 1746, a tobacconist and guilds-brother of Inverness, died on 29 May 1831, husband of Margaret Shaw, born 1768, died 20 June 1853. [Chapel Yard gravestone, Inverness]

TULLOCH, JAMES, master of the Resolution of Inverness trading with Fort William in 1811. [NRS.E504.17.8]

TULLOCH, JOHN, a merchant in Inverness, died 2 February 1847, husband of Grace Fraser. [Chapel Yard gravestone, Inverness]

TULLOCH, ROBERT, in Campbellton, Fort George, a letter in 1835, [NRS.GD23.6.702]; sequestration, 1844. [NRS.CS279.2600]

TYTLER, GEORGE GRANT FRASER, eldest son of William Fraser Tytler of Balnain and Bursyards, the Sheriff of Inverness, was drowned on 12 March 1836 when on passage home aboard the Hercules from Van Diemen's Land, [Tasmania]. [AJ.4616]

URQUHART, ALEXANDER, born 1768, died 9 May 1838. [Chapel Yard gravestone, Inverness]

URQUHART, GEORGE, an upholsterer in Inverness, 1810. [NRS.CS36.1.97]

URQUHART, or HOSSACK, ISABELLA, born 1787 in Resolis, a servant now a pauper in Shoe Street, Merkinch, in 1857. [IPR]

URQUHART, JAMES, born 1816, a builder, died 18 January 1857, husband of Margaret MacKenzie, born 1818, died in Glasgow on 30 July 1902. [Chapel Yard gravestone, Inverness]

URQUHART, JOHN, a coachmaker from Inverness, emigrated to Australia in 1828, died in Sydney, New South Wales, on 28 October 1840. [AJ.4867]

URQUHART, LEONARD, a mason in Inverness, died in June 1847, husband of Helen Mackenzie, who died on 2 March 1876. [Old High gravestone, Inverness]. [Chapel Yard gravestone, Inverness]

URQUHART, WILLIAM, born 1830, a merchant in Inverness, died 26 May 1892, husband of Catherine Clark, born 1834, died 16 December 1899.

VASS, JOHANNA, born 1809 in Inverness, a pauper in Academy Street, Inverness, in 1857. [IPR]

VASS, JOHN, born 1715, tacksman of the Kirktown of Daviot, died in 1802, husband of Margaret McIntosh, born 1724, died in 1810. [Daviot gravestone]

WALKER, CHRISTY, widow of Alexander McGregor in Laggan, a petition in 1832. [NRS.GD112.11.9.8.8]

WALKER, HENRY, from Inverness, graduated MA from King's College, Aberdeen, in March 1837. [KCA]

WARBY, WILLIAM, a vintner in Inverness, 1814. [NRS.CS36.9.71]

WELLS, JOHN, born 1810, of Drumnadrochit, died 1 May 1860, husband of Elizabeth Ross, who died on 11 December 1870. [Chapel Yard gravestone, Inverness]

WELSH, JAMES, from Inverness, graduated MA from King's College, Aberdeen, on 30 March 1807. [KCA]

WELSH, WILLIAM, of Millburn, born 1737, a merchant in Inverness, died 8 January 1816, husband of Marjory Alves, born 1744, died 2 April 1793. [Chapel Yard gravestone, Inverness]

WHYTE, DONALD, born 1806, a teacher at Culaird, died 14 May 1883, husband of Catherine McNaughton, born 1807, died 20 June 1856, parents of Donald Whyte, born 1836, who was killed at the Siege of Sebastipol, Crimea, Russia, on 17 April 1855. [Dores gravestone]

WHYTE, HELEN, eldest daughter of Reverend James Whyte in New York, died in Telford Street, Inverness, on 1 January 1844. [AJ.5019]

WILLIAMS, WILLIAM, former barrack master at Fort George, 1836. [NRS.E886/60]

WILLIAMSON, DAVID, son of Robert Williamson a merchant in Inverness, was educated at Marischal College in Aberdeen in 1849. [MCA]

WILSON, ALEXANDER, a merchant in Inverness, father of James F. Wilson born 1789, settled in New Orleans, Louisiana, died in Virginia on 5 October 1821. [EEC.17257] [IJ.3866]

WILSON, ALICK NEWTON, son of James Wilson a banker in Inverness, was educated at Marischal College around 1855. [MCA]

WILSON, JAMES F., born 1789, eldest son of Alexander Wilson a merchant in Inverness, settled in New Orleans, Louisiana, died in Virginia on 5 October 1821. [BM.40.263][DPCA][AJ.3866]EEC.17257]

WILSON, JAMES, born 27 January 1804, died 2 August 1870. [Chapel Yard gravestone, Inverness]

WILSON, JAMES, born 18 March 1837 in Inverness, third son of James and Isabella Wilson, graduated MA from Jesus College, Cambridge, Rector of Barking, Suffolk, died there on 7 September 1904. [Chapel Yard gravestone, Inverness]

WILSON, LILIAS, daughter of Alexander Wilson a merchant in Inverness, married Alexander Robertson, a surgeon from Jamaica, on 25 October 1802. [GM.72.1224]

WIMBERLEY, Captain DOUGLAS, born 11 June 1828, fought in Crimea with the 20th Regiment of Foot, in the Indian Mutiny with 79th Cameron Highlanders, later an Honorary Sheriff Substitute and Justice of the Peace for Inverness, died 7 November 1912. [Old High Church, Inverness]

WINCHESTER, WILLIAM, master of the Culloden of Inverness trading with Fort William in 1811, trading with Ballachulish in1812. [NRS.E504.17.8]

WINTON, ALEXANDER, born 1782 in Auchterless, Aberdeenshire, a farmer at Viewhill of Ardesier for over 52 years, died on 9 December 1864. [Kirkton of Ardersier gravestone]

WISE, JAMES, born in Moniack, a deserter from the 3rd Battalion of the Rifle Brigade, was accused of theft in 1816. [NRS.AD14.16.60]

WISHART, ROBERT, in Dalmaggy, a contract to build a dyke at Daviot House in 1832. [NRS.GD176.1312]

YOUNG, CHARLES CORNELIUS CARDEW, born 1845, son of Colonel John Smith Young of Ness House, Inverness, died 23 December 1922. [Old High Church, Inverness]

YOUNG, Colonel JOHN SMITH, of Ness House, Inverness, born 9 January 1796, died 2 January 1868, husband of Jane Ogilvy Grant, born 23 March 1804, died 21 February 1882, parents of Edward James Young, born 27 May 1842 at the Cape of Good Hope, South Africa, died in Edinburgh on 6 September 1920. [Old High Church, Inverness]

YOUNG, LACHLAN, born 1820, died in Milton of Brachlichan on 27 July 1877, husband of Catherine Cuthbert, born 1819, died 26 May 1906. [Brachlich gravestone]

YOUNG, or PHIMISTER, MARY, born 1772 in Inverness, a widow and a pauper in Grant's Close, Inverness, in 1857. [IPR]

YOUNG, MURDOCH, born 1755, a dyer in Inverness, died on 21 September 1833. [Chapel Yard gravestone, Inverness]

YOUNG, RODERICK, from Demerara, married Jessie MacKay, eldest daughter of Captain MacKay of Skail, in Inverness on 20 June 1810. [SM.73.553]

CPSIA information can be obtained
at www.ICGtesting.com
Printed in the USA
BVHW031458111022
649159BV00013B/912